OTHELLO

OTHELLO

WILLIAM SHAKESPEARE

AMAZON CLASSICS

Published by AmazonClassics, Seattle

www.apub.com

Amazon, the Amazon logo, and AmazonClassics are trademarks of Amazon.com, Inc., or its affiliates.

ISBN-10: 1542047625
ISBN-13: 9781542047623
eISBN: 9781542097628

Series design by Jeff Miller, Faceout Studio

Printed in the United States of America

CONTENTS

PERSONS REPRESENTED

DUKE of Venice.

BRABANTIO, a Senator.

Other Senators.

GRATIANO, Brother to Brabantio.

LODOVICO, Kinsman to Brabantio.

OTHELLO, a noble Moor, in the service of Venice.

CASSIO, his Lieutenant.

IAGO, his Ancient.

MONTANO, Othello's predecessor in the government of Cyprus.

RODERIGO, a Venetian Gentleman.

CLOWN, Servant to Othello.

HERALD.

DESDEMONA, Daughter to Brabantio and Wife to Othello.

EMILIA, Wife to Iago.

BIANCA, Mistress to Cassio.

OFFICERS, GENTLEMEN, MESSENGER, MUSICIANS, HERALD, SAILOR, ATTENDANTS, &C.

SCENE—The First Act in Venice; during the rest of the Play at a Seaport in Cyprus.

ACT 1.

Scene 1. Venice. A street.

*[Enter **Roderigo** and **Iago**.]*

Roderigo
Tush, never tell me; I take it much unkindly
That thou, Iago, who hast had my purse
As if the strings were thine, shouldst know of this,—

Iago
'Sblood, but you will not hear me:—
5   If ever I did dream of such a matter,
Abhor me.

Roderigo
Thou told'st me thou didst hold him in thy hate.

Iago
Despise me, if I do not. Three great ones of the city,
In personal suit to make me his lieutenant,
10   Off-capp'd to him:—and, by the faith of man,
I know my price, I am worth no worse a place:—
But he, as loving his own pride and purposes,
Evades them, with a bumbast circumstance

Horribly stuff'd with epithets of war:
15 And, in conclusion, nonsuits
My mediators: for, "Certes," says he,
"I have already chose my officer."
And what was he?
Forsooth, a great arithmetician,
20 One Michael Cassio, a Florentine,
A fellow almost damn'd in a fair wife;
That never set a squadron in the field,
Nor the division of a battle knows
More than a spinster; unless the bookish theoric,
25 Wherein the toged consuls can propose
As masterly as he: mere prattle, without practice,
Is all his soldiership. But he, sir, had the election:
And I,—of whom his eyes had seen the proof
At Rhodes, at Cyprus, and on other grounds,
30 Christian and heathen,—must be belee'd and calm'd
By debitor and creditor, this counter-caster;
He, in good time, must his lieutenant be,
And I—God bless the mark! his Moorship's ancient.

RODERIGO
By heaven, I rather would have been his hangman.

IAGO
35 Why, there's no remedy; 'tis the curse of service,
Preferment goes by letter and affection,
And not by old gradation, where each second
Stood heir to the first. Now, sir, be judge yourself
Whether I in any just term am affin'd
40 To love the Moor.

RODERIGO

I would not follow him, then.

IAGO

O, sir, content you;
I follow him to serve my turn upon him:
We cannot all be masters, nor all masters
45 Cannot be truly follow'd. You shall mark
Many a duteous and knee-crooking knave
That, doting on his own obsequious bondage,
Wears out his time, much like his master's ass,
For nought but provender; and when he's old, cashier'd:
50 Whip me such honest knaves. Others there are
Who, trimm'd in forms and visages of duty,
Keep yet their hearts attending on themselves;
And, throwing but shows of service on their lords,
Do well thrive by them, and when they have lin'd their
55 coats,
Do themselves homage: these fellows have some soul;
And such a one do I profess myself. For, sir,
It is as sure as you are Roderigo,
Were I the Moor, I would not be Iago:
60 In following him, I follow but myself;
Heaven is my judge, not I for love and duty,
But seeming so for my peculiar end:
For when my outward action doth demonstrate
The native act and figure of my heart
65 In complement extern, 'tis not long after
But I will wear my heart upon my sleeve
For daws to peck at: I am not what I am.

RODERIGO
What a full fortune does the thick lips owe,
If he can carry't thus!

IAGO
70 Call up her father,
Rouse him:—make after him, poison his delight,
Proclaim him in the streets; incense her kinsmen,
And, though he in a fertile climate dwell,
Plague him with flies: though that his joy be joy,
75 Yet throw such changes of vexation on't
As it may lose some color.

RODERIGO
Here is her father's house: I'll call aloud.

IAGO
Do; with like timorous accent and dire yell
As when, by night and negligence, the fire
80 Is spied in populous cities.

RODERIGO
What, ho, Brabantio! Signior Brabantio, ho!

IAGO
Awake! what, ho, Brabantio! thieves! thieves! thieves!
Look to your house, your daughter, and your bags!
Thieves! thieves!

[**BRABANTIO** *appears above at a window.*]

BRABANTIO

85 What is the reason of this terrible summons?
What is the matter there?

RODERIGO

Signior, is all your family within?

IAGO

Are your doors locked?

BRABANTIO

Why, wherefore ask you this?

IAGO

90 Zounds, sir, you're robb'd; for shame, put on your gown;
Your heart is burst, you have lost half your soul;
Even now, now, very now, an old black ram
Is tupping your white ewe. Arise, arise;
Awake the snorting citizens with the bell,
95 Or else the devil will make a grandsire of you:
Arise, I say.

BRABANTIO

What, have you lost your wits?

RODERIGO

Most reverend signior, do you know my voice?

BRABANTIO

Not I; what are you?

RODERIGO

100   My name is Roderigo.

BRABANTIO

The worser welcome:
I have charged thee not to haunt about my doors;
In honest plainness thou hast heard me say
My daughter is not for thee; and now, in madness,
105   Being full of supper and distempering draughts,
Upon malicious bravery dost thou come
To start my quiet.

RODERIGO

Sir, sir, sir,—

BRABANTIO

But thou must needs be sure
110   My spirit and my place have in them power
To make this bitter to thee.

RODERIGO

Patience, good sir.

BRABANTIO

What tell'st thou me of robbing? this is Venice;
My house is not a grange.

RODERIGO

115   Most grave Brabantio,
In simple and pure soul I come to you.

IAGO

Zounds, sir, you are one of those that will not serve God
if the devil bid you. Because we come to do you service,
and you think we are ruffians, you'll have your daughter
120 covered with a Barbary horse; you'll have your nephews
neigh to you; you'll have coursers for cousins and gennets
for germans.

BRABANTIO

What profane wretch art thou?

IAGO

I am one, sir, that comes to tell you your daughter and the
125 Moor are now making the beast with two backs.

BRABANTIO

Thou art a villain.

IAGO

You are—a senator.

BRABANTIO

This thou shalt answer; I know thee, Roderigo.

RODERIGO

Sir, I will answer anything. But, I beseech you,
130 If 't be your pleasure and most wise consent,—
As partly I find it is,—that your fair daughter,
At this odd-even and dull watch o' the night,
Transported with no worse nor better guard
But with a knave of common hire, a gondolier,
135 To the gross clasps of a lascivious Moor,—

If this be known to you, and your allowance,
We then have done you bold and saucy wrongs;
But if you know not this, my manners tell me
We have your wrong rebuke. Do not believe
140 That, from the sense of all civility,
I thus would play and trifle with your reverence:
Your daughter,—if you have not given her leave,—
I say again, hath made a gross revolt;
Tying her duty, beauty, wit, and fortunes
145 In an extravagant and wheeling stranger
Of here and everywhere. Straight satisfy yourself:
If she be in her chamber or your house
Let loose on me the justice of the state
For thus deluding you.

BRABANTIO
150 Strike on the tinder, ho!
Give me a taper!—Call up all my people!—
This accident is not unlike my dream:
Belief of it oppresses me already.—
Light, I say! light!

[*Exit from above.*]

IAGO
155 Farewell; for I must leave you:
It seems not meet nor wholesome to my place
To be produc'd,—as if I stay I shall,—
Against the Moor: for I do know the state,—
However this may gall him with some check,—
160 Cannot with safety cast him; for he's embark'd

With such loud reason to the Cyprus wars,—
Which even now stand in act,—that, for their souls,
Another of his fathom they have none
To lead their business: in which regard,
165 Though I do hate him as I do hell pains,
Yet, for necessity of present life,
I must show out a flag and sign of love,
Which is indeed but sign. That you shall surely find him,
Lead to the Sagittary the raisèd search;
170 And there will I be with him. So, farewell.

[*Exit.*]

[*Enter, below,* BRABANTIO, *and* SERVANTS *with torches.*]

BRABANTIO
It is too true an evil: gone she is;
And what's to come of my despisèd time
Is naught but bitterness.—Now, Roderigo,
Where didst thou see her?—O unhappy girl!—
175 With the Moor, say'st thou?—Who would be a father!
How didst thou know 'twas she?—O, she deceives me
Past thought.—What said she to you?—Get more tapers;
Raise all my kindred.—Are they married, think you?

RODERIGO
Truly, I think they are.

BRABANTIO
180 O heaven!—How got she out?—O treason of the blood!—
Fathers, from hence trust not your daughters' minds
By what you see them act.—Are there not charms

By which the property of youth and maidhood
May be abused? Have you not read, Roderigo,
185 Of some such thing?

RODERIGO
Yes, sir, I have indeed.

BRABANTIO
Call up my brother.—O, would you had had her!—
Some one way, some another.—Do you know
Where we may apprehend her and the Moor?

RODERIGO
190 I think I can discover him, if you please
To get good guard, and go along with me.

BRABANTIO
Pray you, lead on. At every house I'll call;
I may command at most.—Get weapons, ho!
And raise some special officers of night.—
195 On, good Roderigo:—I'll deserve your pains.

[Exeunt.]

SCENE 2. VENICE. ANOTHER STREET.

[Enter **OTHELLO**, **IAGO**, *and* **ATTENDANTS** *with torches.]*

IAGO
Though in the trade of war I have slain men,
Yet do I hold it very stuff o' the conscience
To do no contrivèd murder: I lack iniquity

Sometimes to do me service: nine or ten times
5   I had thought to have yerk'd him here under the ribs.

OTHELLO
'Tis better as it is.

IAGO
Nay, but he prated,
And spoke such scurvy and provoking terms
Against your honor,
10   That, with the little godliness I have,
I did full hard forbear him. But, I pray you, sir,
Are you fast married? Be assured of this,
That the magnifico is much beloved;
And hath, in his effect, a voice potential
15   As double as the duke's: he will divorce you;
Or put upon you what restraint and grievance
The law,—with all his might to enforce it on,—
Will give him cable.

OTHELLO
Let him do his spite:
20   My services which I have done the signiory
Shall out-tongue his complaints. 'Tis yet to know,—
Which, when I know that boasting is an honor,
I shall promulgate,—I fetch my life and being
From men of royal siege; and my demerits
25   May speak unbonneted to as proud a fortune
As this that I have reach'd: for know, Iago,
But that I love the gentle Desdemona,
I would not my unhousèd free condition
Put into circumscription and confine

30   For the sea's worth. But, look! what lights come yond?

IAGO
Those are the raisèd father and his friends:
You were best go in.

OTHELLO
Not I; I must be found;
My parts, my title, and my perfect soul
35   Shall manifest me rightly. Is it they?

IAGO
By Janus, I think no.

[*Enter* **CASSIO** *and certain* **OFFICERS** *with torches.*]

OTHELLO
The servants of the duke and my lieutenant.—
The goodness of the night upon you, friends!
What is the news?

CASSIO
40   The duke does greet you, general;
And he requires your haste-post-haste appearance
Even on the instant.

OTHELLO
What is the matter, think you?

CASSIO
Something from Cyprus, as I may divine:
45   It is a business of some heat: the galleys

Have sent a dozen sequent messengers
This very night at one another's heels;
And many of the consuls, rais'd and met,
Are at the duke's already: you have been hotly call'd for;
50 When, being not at your lodging to be found,
The senate hath sent about three several quests
To search you out.

OTHELLO
'Tis well I am found by you.
I will but spend a word here in the house,
55 And go with you.

[*Exit.*]

CASSIO
Ancient, what makes he here?

IAGO
Faith, he to-night hath boarded a land carack:
If it prove lawful prize, he's made forever.

CASSIO
I do not understand.

IAGO
60 He's married.

CASSIO
To who?

[*Re-enter* **OTHELLO**.]

IAGO
Marry, to—Come, captain, will you go?

OTHELLO
Have with you.

CASSIO
Here comes another troop to seek for you.

IAGO
65 It is Brabantio.—General, be advis'd;
He comes to bad intent.

[*Enter* **BRABANTIO**, **RODERIGO**, *and* **OFFICERS** *with torches and weapons.*]

OTHELLO
Holla! stand there!

RODERIGO
Signior, it is the Moor.

BRABANTIO
Down with him, thief!

[*They draw on both sides.*]

IAGO
70 You, Roderigo! come, sir, I am for you.

OTHELLO
Keep up your bright swords, for the dew will rust them.—

Good signior, you shall more command with years
Than with your weapons.

BRABANTIO
O thou foul thief, where hast thou stow'd my daughter?
75 Damn'd as thou art, thou hast enchanted her;
For I'll refer me to all things of sense,
If she in chains of magic were not bound,
Whether a maid so tender, fair, and happy,
So opposite to marriage that she shunn'd
80 The wealthy curlèd darlings of our nation,
Would ever have, to incur a general mock,
Run from her guardage to the sooty bosom
Of such a thing as thou,—to fear, not to delight.
Judge me the world, if 'tis not gross in sense
85 That thou hast practis'd on her with foul charms;
Abus'd her delicate youth with drugs or minerals
That weaken motion:—I'll have't disputed on;
'Tis probable, and palpable to thinking.
I therefore apprehend and do attach thee
90 For an abuser of the world, a practiser
Of arts inhibited and out of warrant.—
Lay hold upon him: if he do resist,
Subdue him at his peril.

OTHELLO
Hold your hands,
95 Both you of my inclining and the rest:
Were it my cue to fight, I should have known it
Without a prompter.—Where will you that I go
To answer this your charge?

BRABANTIO

To prison; till fit time
100 Of law and course of direct session
Call thee to answer.

OTHELLO

What if I do obey?
How may the duke be therewith satisfied,
Whose messengers are here about my side,
105 Upon some present business of the state,
To bring me to him?

FIRST OFFICER

'Tis true, most worthy signior;
The duke's in council, and your noble self,
I am sure, is sent for.

BRABANTIO

110 How! the duke in council!
In this time of the night!—Bring him away:
Mine's not an idle cause: the duke himself,
Or any of my brothers of the state,
Cannot but feel this wrong as 'twere their own;
115 For if such actions may have passage free,
Bond slaves and pagans shall our statesmen be.

[*Exeunt.*]

SCENE 3. VENICE. A COUNCIL CHAMBER.

[*The* **DUKE** *and* **SENATORS** *sitting at a table;* **OFFICERS** *attending.*]

DUKE

There is no composition in these news
That gives them credit.

FIRST SENATOR

Indeed, they are disproportion'd;
My letters say a hundred and seven galleys.

DUKE

5 And mine a hundred and forty.

SECOND SENATOR

And mine two hundred:
But though they jump not on a just account,—
As in these cases, where the aim reports,
'Tis oft with difference,—yet do they all confirm
10 A Turkish fleet, and bearing up to Cyprus.

DUKE

Nay, it is possible enough to judgement:
I do not so secure me in the error,
But the main article I do approve
In fearful sense.

SAILOR

15 [*Within.*] What, ho! what, ho! what, ho!

FIRST OFFICER

A messenger from the galleys.

[*Enter a* **SAILOR.**]

DUKE
Now,—what's the business?

SAILOR
The Turkish preparation makes for Rhodes;
So was I bid report here to the state
20 By Signior Angelo.

DUKE
How say you by this change?

FIRST SENATOR
This cannot be,
By no assay of reason: 'tis a pageant
To keep us in false gaze. When we consider
25 The importancy of Cyprus to the Turk;
And let ourselves again but understand
That, as it more concerns the Turk than Rhodes,
So may he with more facile question bear it,
For that it stands not in such warlike brace,
30 But altogether lacks the abilities
That Rhodes is dress'd in. If we make thought of this,
We must not think the Turk is so unskilful
To leave that latest which concerns him first;
Neglecting an attempt of ease and gain,
35 To wake and wage a danger profitless.

DUKE
Nay, in all confidence, he's not for Rhodes.

FIRST OFFICER
Here is more news.

[*Enter a* MESSENGER.]

MESSENGER
The Ottomites, reverend and gracious,
Steering with due course toward the isle of Rhodes,
40 Have there injointed them with an after fleet.

FIRST SENATOR
Ay, so I thought.—How many, as you guess?

MESSENGER
Of thirty sail: and now they do re-stem
Their backward course, bearing with frank appearance
Their purposes toward Cyprus.—Signior Montano,
45 Your trusty and most valiant servitor,
With his free duty recommends you thus,
And prays you to believe him.

DUKE
'Tis certain, then, for Cyprus.—
Marcus Luccicos, is not he in town?

FIRST SENATOR
50 He's now in Florence.

DUKE
Write from us to him; post-post-haste despatch.

FIRST SENATOR
Here comes Brabantio and the valiant Moor.

[*Enter* BRABANTIO, OTHELLO, IAGO, RODERIGO, *and* OFFICERS.]

DUKE
Valiant Othello, we must straight employ you
Against the general enemy Ottoman.—
55 [*To* **BRABANTIO**.] I did not see you; welcome, gentle
signior;
We lack'd your counsel and your help to-night.

BRABANTIO
So did I yours. Good your grace, pardon me;
Neither my place, nor aught I heard of business
Hath rais'd me from my bed; nor doth the general care
60 Take hold on me; for my particular grie
Is of so flood-gate and o'erbearing nature
That it engluts and swallows other sorrows,
And it is still itself.

DUKE
Why, what's the matter?

BRABANTIO
65 My daughter! O, my daughter!

DUKE AND SENATORS
Dead?

BRABANTIO
Ay, to me;
She is abused, stol'n from me, and corrupted
By spells and medicines bought of mountebanks;
70 For nature so preposterously to err,
Being not deficient, blind, or lame of sense,
Sans witchcraft could not.

DUKE

Whoe'er he be that, in this foul proceeding,
Hath thus beguiled your daughter of herself,
75　And you of her, the bloody book of law
You shall yourself read in the bitter letter
After your own sense; yea, though our proper son
Stood in your action.

BRABANTIO

Humbly I thank your grace.
80　Here is the man, this Moor; whom now, it seems,
Your special mandate for the state affairs
Hath hither brought.

DUKE AND SENATORS

We are very sorry for't.

DUKE

[*To* **OTHELLO**.] What, in your own part, can you say to this?

BRABANTIO

85　Nothing, but this is so.

OTHELLO

Most potent, grave, and reverend signiors,
My very noble and approv'd good masters,—
That I have ta'en away this old man's daughter,
It is most true; true, I have married her:
90　The very head and front of my offending
Hath this extent, no more. Rude am I in my speech,
And little bless'd with the soft phrase of peace;

For since these arms of mine had seven years' pith,
Till now some nine moons wasted, they have us'd
95 Their dearest action in the tented field;
And little of this great world can I speak,
More than pertains to feats of broil and battle;
And therefore little shall I grace my cause
In speaking for myself. Yet, by your gracious patience,
100 I will a round unvarnish'd tale deliver
Of my whole course of love: what drugs, what charms,
What conjuration, and what mighty magic,—
For such proceeding I am charged withal,—
I won his daughter.

BRABANTIO

105 A maiden never bold:
Of spirit so still and quiet that her motion
Blush'd at herself; and she,—in spite of nature,
Of years, of country, credit, everything,—
To fall in love with what she fear'd to look on!
110 It is judgement maim'd and most imperfect
That will confess perfection so could err
Against all rules of nature; and must be driven
To find out practices of cunning hell,
Why this should be. I therefore vouch again,
115 That with some mixtures powerful o'er the blood,
Or with some dram conjur'd to this effect,
He wrought upon her.

DUKE

To vouch this is no proof;
Without more wider and more overt test
120 Than these thin habits and poor likelihoods

Of modern seeming do prefer against him.

FIRST SENATOR
But, Othello, speak:
Did you by indirect and forcèd courses
Subdue and poison this young maid's affections?
125 Or came it by request, and such fair question
As soul to soul affordeth?

OTHELLO
I do beseech you,
Send for the lady to the Sagittary,
And let her speak of me before her father.
130 If you do find me foul in her report,
The trust, the office I do hold of you,
Not only take away, but let your sentence
Even fall upon my life.

DUKE
Fetch Desdemona hither.

OTHELLO
135 Ancient, conduct them; you best know the place.—

[*Exeunt* **IAGO** *and* **ATTENDANTS**.]

And, till she come, as truly as to heaven
I do confess the vices of my blood,
So justly to your grave ears I'll present
How I did thrive in this fair lady's love,
140 And she in mine.

DUKE
Say it, Othello.

OTHELLO
Her father lov'd me; oft invited me;
Still question'd me the story of my life,
From year to year,—the battles, sieges, fortunes,
145 That I have pass'd.
I ran it through, even from my boyish days
To the very moment that he bade me tell it:
Wherein I spake of most disastrous chances,
Of moving accidents by flood and field;
150 Of hair-breadth scapes i' the imminent deadly breach;
Of being taken by the insolent foe,
And sold to slavery; of my redemption thence,
And portance in my travels' history:
Wherein of antres vast and deserts idle,
155 Rough quarries, rocks, and hills whose heads touch heaven,
It was my hint to speak,—such was the process;
And of the Cannibals that each other eat,
The Anthropophagi, and men whose heads
Do grow beneath their shoulders. This to hear
160 Would Desdemona seriously incline:
But still the house affairs would draw her thence;
Which ever as she could with haste despatch,
She'd come again, and with a greedy ear
Devour up my discourse; which I observing,
165 Took once a pliant hour; and found good means
To draw from her a prayer of earnest heart
That I would all my pilgrimage dilate,
Whereof by parcels she had something heard,
But not intentively; I did consent;

170 And often did beguile her of her tears,
When I did speak of some distressful stroke
That my youth suffer'd. My story being done,
She gave me for my pains a world of sighs:
She swore,—in faith, 'twas strange, 'twas passing strange;
175 'Twas pitiful, 'twas wondrous pitiful:
She wish'd she had not heard it, yet she wish'd
That heaven had made her such a man: she thank'd me;
And bade me, if I had a friend that lov'd her,
I should but teach him how to tell my story,
180 And that would woo her. Upon this hint I spake:
She lov'd me for the dangers I had pass'd;
And I lov'd her that she did pity them.
This only is the witchcraft I have us'd:—
Here comes the lady; let her witness it.

[*Enter* DESDEMONA, IAGO, *and* ATTENDANTS.]

DUKE

185 I think this tale would win my daughter too.—
Good Brabantio,
Take up this mangled matter at the best.
Men do their broken weapons rather use
Than their bare hands.

BRABANTIO

190 I pray you, hear her speak:
If she confess that she was half the wooer,
Destruction on my head, if my bad blame
Light on the man!—Come hither, gentle mistress:
Do you perceive in all this noble company
195 Where most you owe obedience?

DESDEMONA
My noble father,
I do perceive here a divided duty:
To you I am bound for life and education;
My life and education both do learn me
200 How to respect you; you are the lord of duty,—
I am hitherto your daughter: but here's my husband;
And so much duty as my mother show'd
To you, preferring you before her father,
So much I challenge that I may profess
205 Due to the Moor, my lord.

BRABANTIO
God be with you!—I have done.—
Please it your grace, on to the state affairs:
I had rather to adopt a child than get it.—
Come hither, Moor:
210 I here do give thee that with all my heart
Which, but thou hast already, with all my heart
I would keep from thee.—For your sake, jewel,
I am glad at soul I have no other child;
For thy escape would teach me tyranny,
215 To hang clogs on them.—I have done, my lord.

DUKE
Let me speak like yourself; and lay a sentence
Which, as a grise or step, may help these lovers
Into your favour.
When remedies are past, the griefs are ended
220 By seeing the worst, which late on hopes depended.
To mourn a mischief that is past and gone
Is the next way to draw new mischief on.

What cannot be preserved when fortune takes,
Patience her injury a mockery makes.
225   The robb'd that smiles steals something from the thief;
He robs himself that spends a bootless grief.

Brabantio
So let the Turk of Cyprus us beguile;
We lose it not so long as we can smile;
He bears the sentence well, that nothing bears
230   But the free comfort which from thence he hears;
But he bears both the sentence and the sorrow
That, to pay grief, must of poor patience borrow.
These sentences, to sugar or to gall,
Being strong on both sides, are equivocal:
235   But words are words; I never yet did hear
That the bruis'd heart was piercèd through the ear.—
I humbly beseech you, proceed to the affairs of state.

Duke
The Turk with a most mighty preparation makes for
Cyprus.—Othello, the fortitude of the place is best known to
240   you; and though we have there a substitute of most allowed
sufficiency, yet opinion, a sovereign mistress of effects, throws
a more safer voice on you: you must therefore be content to
slubber the gloss of your new fortunes with this more stub-
born and boisterous expedition.

Othello
245   The tyrant custom, most grave senators,
Hath made the flinty and steel couch of war
My thrice-driven bed of down: I do agnize
A natural and prompt alacrity

I find in hardness; and do undertake
250 These present wars against the Ottomites.
Most humbly, therefore, bending to your state,
I crave fit disposition for my wife;
Due reference of place and exhibition;
With such accommodation and besort
255 As levels with her breeding.

DUKE
If you please,
Be't at her father's.

BRABANTIO
I'll not have it so.

OTHELLO
Nor I.

DESDEMONA
260 Nor I. I would not there reside,
To put my father in impatient thoughts,
By being in his eye. Most gracious duke,
To my unfolding lend your prosperous ear;
And let me find a charter in your voice
265 To assist my simpleness.

DUKE
What would you, Desdemona?

DESDEMONA
That I did love the Moor to live with him,

My downright violence and storm of fortunes
May trumpet to the world: my heart's subdu'd
270 Even to the very quality of my lord:
I saw Othello's visage in his mind;
And to his honors and his valiant parts
Did I my soul and fortunes consecrate.
So that, dear lords, if I be left behind,
275 A moth of peace, and he go to the war,
The rites for which I love him are bereft me,
And I a heavy interim shall support
By his dear absence. Let me go with him.

OTHELLO
Let her have your voices.
280 Vouch with me, heaven, I therefore beg it not
To please the palate of my appetite;
Nor to comply with heat,—the young affects
In me defunct,—and proper satisfaction;
But to be free and bounteous to her mind:
285 And heaven defend your good souls, that you think
I will your serious and great business scant
For she is with me: no, when light-wing'd toys
Of feather'd Cupid seel with wanton dullness
My speculative and offic'd instruments,
290 That my disports corrupt and taint my business,
Let housewives make a skillet of my helm,
And all indign and base adversities
Make head against my estimation!

DUKE
Be it as you shall privately determine,
295 Either for her stay or going: the affair cries haste,

And speed must answer it.

FIRST SENATOR
You must away to-night.

OTHELLO
With all my heart.

DUKE
At nine i' the morning here we'll meet again.—
300   Othello, leave some officer behind,
And he shall our commission bring to you;
With such things else of quality and respect
As doth import you.

OTHELLO
So please your grace, my ancient,—
305   A man he is of honesty and trust,—
To his conveyance I assign my wife,
With what else needful your good grace shall think
To be sent after me.

DUKE
Let it be so.—
310   Good night to everyone.— [*To* **BRABANTIO**.] And, noble
signior,
If virtue no delighted beauty lack,
Your son-in-law is far more fair than black.

FIRST SENATOR
Adieu, brave Moor; use Desdemona well.

BRABANTIO

315 Look to her, Moor, if thou hast eyes to see:
She has deceiv'd her father, and may thee.

[*Exeunt* DUKE, SENATORS, OFFICERS. *&c.*]

OTHELLO

My life upon her faith!—Honest Iago,
My Desdemona must I leave to thee:
I pr'ythee, let thy wife attend on her;
320 And bring them after in the best advantage.—
Come, Desdemona, I have but an hour
Of love, of worldly matters and direction,
To spend with thee: we must obey the time.

[*Exeunt* OTHELLO *and* DESDEMONA.]

RODERIGO

Iago,—

IAGO

325 What say'st thou, noble heart?

RODERIGO

What will I do, thinkest thou?

IAGO

Why, go to bed and sleep.

RODERIGO

I will incontinently drown myself.

IAGO

330 If thou dost, I shall never love thee after. Why, thou silly gentleman!

RODERIGO

It is silliness to live when to live is torment; and then have we a prescription to die when death is our physician.

IAGO

O villainous! I have looked upon the world for four times seven years, and since I could distinguish betwixt a benefit
335 and an injury, I never found man that knew how to love himself. Ere I would say I would drown myself for the love of a Guinea-hen, I would change my humanity with a baboon.

RODERIGO

What should I do? I confess it is my shame to be so fond, but it is not in my virtue to amend it.

IAGO

340 Virtue! a fig! 'Tis in ourselves that we are thus or thus. Our bodies are gardens, to the which our wills are gardeners; so that if we will plant nettles or sow lettuce, set hyssop and weed up thyme, supply it with one gender of herbs or distract it with many, either to have it sterile with idleness
345 or manured with industry; why, the power and corrigible authority of this lies in our wills. If the balance of our lives had not one scale of reason to poise another of sensuality, the blood and baseness of our natures would conduct us to most preposterous conclusions: But we have reason to cool
350 our raging motions, our carnal stings, our unbitted lusts; whereof I take this, that you call love, to be a sect or scion.

RODERIGO

It cannot be.

IAGO

It is merely a lust of the blood and a permission of the will. Come, be a man: drown thyself! drown cats and blind
355 puppies. I have professed me thy friend, and I confess me knit to thy deserving with cables of perdurable toughness; I could never better stead thee than now. Put money in thy purse; follow thou the wars; defeat thy favour with an usurped beard; I say, put money in thy purse. It cannot
360 be that Desdemona should long continue her love to the Moor,—put money in thy purse,—nor he his to her: it was a violent commencement, and thou shalt see an answerable sequestration;—put but money in thy purse.—These Moors are changeable in their wills:—fill thy purse with
365 money: the food that to him now is as luscious as locusts shall be to him shortly as acerb as the coloquintida. She must change for youth: when she is sated with his body, she will find the error of her choice: she must have change, she must: therefore put money in thy purse.—If thou wilt
370 needs damn thyself, do it a more delicate way than drowning. Make all the money thou canst; if sanctimony and a frail vow betwixt an erring barbarian and a supersubtle Venetian be not too hard for my wits and all the tribe of hell, thou shalt enjoy her; therefore make money. A
375 pox of drowning thyself! it is clean out of the way: seek thou rather to be hanged in compassing thy joy than to be drowned and go without her.

RODERIGO

Wilt thou be fast to my hopes, if I depend on the issue?

IAGO

Thou art sure of me:—go, make money:—I have told thee
380 often, and I re-tell thee again and again, I hate the Moor: my
cause is hearted; thine hath no less reason. Let us be conjunc-
tive in our revenge against him: if thou canst cuckold him,
thou dost thyself a pleasure, me a sport. There are many events
in the womb of time which will be delivered. Traverse; go; pro-
385 vide thy money. We will have more of this to-morrow. Adieu.

RODERIGO

Where shall we meet i' the morning?

IAGO

At my lodging.

RODERIGO

I'll be with thee betimes.

IAGO

Go to; farewell. Do you hear, Roderigo?

RODERIGO
390 What say you?

IAGO

No more of drowning, do you hear?

RODERIGO

I am changed: I'll go sell all my land.

[*Exit.*]

IAGO

Thus do I ever make my fool my purse;
For I mine own gain'd knowledge should profane
395   If I would time expend with such a snipe
But for my sport and profit. I hate the Moor;
And it is thought abroad that 'twixt my sheets
He has done my office: I know not if 't be true;
But I, for mere suspicion in that kind,
400   Will do as if for surety. He holds me well,
The better shall my purpose work on him.
Cassio's a proper man: let me see now;
To get his place, and to plume up my will
In double knavery,—How, how?—Let's see:—
405   After some time, to abuse Othello's ear
That he is too familiar with his wife:—
He hath a person, and a smooth dispose,
To be suspected; fram'd to make women false.
The Moor is of a free and open nature,
410   That thinks men honest that but seem to be so;
And will as tenderly be led by the nose
As asses are.
I have't;—it is engender'd:—hell and night
Must bring this monstrous birth to the world's light.

[Exit.]

ACT 2.

Scene 1. A seaport in Cyprus. A Platform.

[*Enter* **Montano** *and two* **Gentlemen**.]

Montano
What from the cape can you discern at sea?

First gentleman
Nothing at all: it is a high-wrought flood;
I cannot, 'twixt the heaven and the main,
Descry a sail.

Montano
5 Methinks the wind hath spoke aloud at land;
A fuller blast ne'er shook our battlements:
If it hath ruffian'd so upon the sea,
What ribs of oak, when mountains melt on them,
Can hold the mortise? What shall we hear of this?

Second gentleman
10 A segregation of the Turkish fleet:
For do but stand upon the foaming shore,
The chidden billow seems to pelt the clouds;
The wind-shak'd surge, with high and monstrous main,

Seems to cast water on the burning Bear,
15 And quench the guards of the ever-fixèd pole;
I never did like molestation view
On the enchafèd flood.

MONTANO
If that the Turkish fleet
Be not enshelter'd and embay'd, they are drown'd;
20 It is impossible to bear it out.

[*Enter a third* **GENTLEMAN**.]

THIRD GENTLEMAN
News, lads! our wars are done.
The desperate tempest hath so bang'd the Turks
That their designment halts; a noble ship of Venice
Hath seen a grievous wreck and sufferance
25 On most part of their fleet.

MONTANO
How! is this true?

THIRD GENTLEMAN
The ship is here put in,
A Veronessa; Michael Cassio,
Lieutenant to the warlike Moor Othello,
30 Is come on shore: the Moor himself's at sea,
And is in full commission here for Cyprus.

MONTANO
I am glad on't; 'tis a worthy governor.

Third gentleman
But this same Cassio,—though he speak of comfort
Touching the Turkish loss,—yet he looks sadly,
35 And prays the Moor be safe; for they were parted
With foul and violent tempest.

Montano
Pray heavens he be;
For I have serv'd him, and the man commands
Like a full soldier. Let's to the sea-side, ho!
40 As well to see the vessel that's come in
As to throw out our eyes for brave Othello,
Even till we make the main and the aerial blue
An indistinct regard.

Third gentleman
Come, let's do so;
45 For every minute is expectancy
Of more arrivance.

[Enter Cassio.*]*

Cassio
Thanks you, the valiant of this warlike isle,
That so approve the Moor! O, let the heavens
Give him defence against the elements,
50 For I have lost him on a dangerous sea!

Montano
Is he well shipp'd?

CASSIO

His bark is stoutly timber'd, and his pilot
Of very expert and approv'd allowance;
Therefore my hopes, not surfeited to death,

55 Stand in bold cure.
[*Within.*] A sail, a sail, a sail!

[*Enter a fourth* **GENTLEMAN.**]

CASSIO

What noise?

FOURTH GENTLEMAN

The town is empty; on the brow o' the sea
Stand ranks of people, and they cry, "A sail!"

CASSIO

60 My hopes do shape him for the governor.

[*Guns within.*]

SECOND GENTLEMAN

They do discharge their shot of courtesy:
Our friends at least.

CASSIO

I pray you, sir, go forth,
And give us truth who 'tis that is arriv'd.

SECOND GENTLEMAN

65 I shall.

[*Exit.*]

MONTANO
But, good lieutenant, is your general wiv'd?

CASSIO
Most fortunately: he hath achiev'd a maid
That paragons description and wild fame,
One that excels the quirks of blazoning pens,
70 And in the essential vesture of creation
Does tire the ingener.—

[*Re-enter second* **GENTLEMAN.**]

How now! who has put in?

SECOND GENTLEMAN
'Tis one Iago, ancient to the general.

CASSIO
He has had most favourable and happy speed:
75 Tempests themselves, high seas, and howling winds,
The gutter'd rocks, and congregated sands,—
Traitors ensteep'd to clog the guiltless keel,—
As having sense of beauty, do omit
Their mortal natures, letting go safely by
80 The divine Desdemona.

MONTANO
What is she?

CASSIO

She that I spake of, our great captain's captain,
Left in the conduct of the bold Iago;
Whose footing here anticipates our thoughts
85 A se'nnight's speed.—Great Jove, Othello guard,
And swell his sail with thine own powerful breath,
That he may bless this bay with his tall ship,
Make love's quick pants in Desdemona's arms,
Give renew'd fire to our extincted spirits,
90 And bring all Cyprus comfort!

[*Enter* **DESDEMONA, EMILIA, IAGO, RODERIGO,** *and* **ATTENDANTS.**]

O, behold,
The riches of the ship is come on shore!
Ye men of Cyprus, let her have your knees.—
Hall to thee, lady! and the grace of heaven,
95 Before, behind thee, and on every hand,
Enwheel thee round!

DESDEMONA

I thank you, valiant Cassio.
What tidings can you tell me of my lord?

CASSIO

He is not yet arrived nor know I aught
100 But that he's well, and will be shortly here.

DESDEMONA

O, but I fear—How lost you company?

CASSIO

The great contention of the sea and skies
Parted our fellowship:—but, hark! a sail.
[*Within.*] A sail, a sail!

[*Guns within.*]

SECOND GENTLEMAN

105 They give their greeting to the citadel:
This likewise is a friend.

CASSIO

See for the news.

[*Exit* **GENTLEMAN.**]

Good ancient, you are welcome:—[*To* **EMILIA.**] Welcome,
mistress:—
110 Let it not gall your patience, good Iago,
That I extend my manners; 'tis my breeding
That gives me this bold show of courtesy.

[*Kissing her.*]

IAGO

Sir, would she give you so much of her lips
As of her tongue she oft bestows on me,
115 You'd have enough.

DESDEMONA

Alas, she has no speech.

IAGO
In faith, too much;
I find it still when I have list to sleep:
Marry, before your ladyship, I grant,
120 She puts her tongue a little in her heart,
And chides with thinking.

EMILIA
You have little cause to say so.

IAGO
Come on, come on; you are pictures out of doors,
Bells in your parlours, wild cats in your kitchens,
125 Saints in your injuries, devils being offended,
Players in your housewifery, and housewives in your beds.

DESDEMONA
O, fie upon thee, slanderer!

IAGO
Nay, it is true, or else I am a Turk:
You rise to play, and go to bed to work.

EMILIA
130 You shall not write my praise.

IAGO
No, let me not.

DESDEMONA
What wouldst thou write of me, if thou shouldst praise me?

IAGO

O gentle lady, do not put me to't;
For I am nothing if not critical.

DESDEMONA

135 Come on, assay—There's one gone to the harbor?

IAGO

Ay, madam.

DESDEMONA

I am not merry; but I do beguile
The thing I am, by seeming otherwise.—
Come, how wouldst thou praise me?

IAGO

140 I am about it; but, indeed, my invention
Comes from my pate as birdlime does from frize,—
It plucks out brains and all: but my Muse labours,
And thus she is deliver'd.
If she be fair and wise,—fairness and wit,
145 The one's for use, the other useth it.

DESDEMONA

Well prais'd! How if she be black and witty?

IAGO

If she be black, and thereto have a wit,
She'll find a white that shall her blackness fit.

DESDEMONA

Worse and worse.

EMILIA

150 How if fair and foolish?

IAGO

She never yet was foolish that was fair;
For even her folly help'd her to an heir.

DESDEMONA

These are old fond paradoxes to make fools laugh i' the
alehouse. What miserable praise hast thou for her that's
155 foul and foolish?

IAGO

There's none so foul and foolish thereunto,
But does foul pranks which fair and wise ones do.

DESDEMONA

O heavy ignorance!—thou praisest the worst best. But
what praise couldst thou bestow on a deserving woman
160 indeed,—one that, in the authority of her merit, did justly
put on the vouch of very malice itself?

IAGO

She that was ever fair and never proud;
Had tongue at will and yet was never loud;
Never lack'd gold and yet went never gay;
165 Fled from her wish, and yet said, "Now I may";
She that, being anger'd, her revenge being nigh,
Bade her wrong stay and her displeasure fly;
She that in wisdom never was so frail
To change the cod's head for the salmon's tail;
170 She that could think and ne'er disclose her mind;

See suitors following and not look behind;
She was a wight, if ever such wight were;—

DESDEMONA

To do what?

IAGO

To suckle fools and chronicle small beer.

DESDEMONA

175 O most lame and impotent conclusion!—Do not learn of
him, Emilia, though he be thy husband.—How say you,
Cassio? is he not a most profane and liberal counsellor?

CASSIO

He speaks home, madam: you may relish him more in the
soldier than in the scholar.

IAGO

180 [*Aside.*] He takes her by the palm: ay, well said, whisper:
with as little a web as this will I ensnare as great a fly as
Cassio. Ay, smile upon her, do; I will gyve thee in thine
own courtship. You say true; 'tis so, indeed: if such tricks
as these strip you out of your lieutenantry, it had been
185 better you had not kissed your three fingers so oft, which
now again you are most apt to play the sir in. Very good;
well kissed! an excellent courtesy! 'tis so, indeed. Yet again
your fingers to your lips? Would they were clyster-pipes
for your sake!

[*Trumpet within.*]

190 The Moor! I know his trumpet.

CASSIO
'Tis truly so.

DESDEMONA
Let's meet him, and receive him.

CASSIO
Lo, where he comes!

[*Enter* **OTHELLO** *and* **ATTENDANTS.**]

OTHELLO
O my fair warrior!

DESDEMONA
195 My dear Othello!

OTHELLO
It gives me wonder great as my content
To see you here before me. O my soul's joy!
If after every tempest come such calms,
May the winds blow till they have waken'd death!
200 And let the laboring bark climb hills of seas
Olympus-high, and duck again as low
As hell's from heaven! If it were now to die,
'Twere now to be most happy; for, I fear,
My soul hath her content so absolute
205 That not another comfort like to this
Succeeds in unknown fate.

DESDEMONA
The heavens forbid
But that our loves and comforts should increase
Even as our days do grow!

OTHELLO
210 Amen to that, sweet powers!—
I cannot speak enough of this content;
It stops me here; it is too much of joy:
And this, and this, the greatest discords be [*Kissing her.*]
That e'er our hearts shall make!

IAGO
215 [*Aside.*] O, you are well tun'd now!
But I'll set down the pegs that make this music,
As honest as I am.

OTHELLO
Come, let us to the castle.—
News, friends; our wars are done, the Turks are drown'd.
220 How does my old acquaintance of this isle?
Honey, you shall be well desir'd in Cyprus;
I have found great love amongst them. O my sweet
I prattle out of fashion, and I dote
In mine own comforts.—I pry'thee, good Iago,
225 Go to the bay and disembark my coffers:
Bring thou the master to the citadel;
He is a good one, and his worthiness
Does challenge much respect.—Come, Desdemona,
Once more well met at Cyprus.

[*Exeunt* OTHELLO, DESDEMONA, *and* ATTENDANTS.]

IAGO

230 Do thou meet me presently at the harbour. Come hither.
If thou be'st valiant,—as, they say, base men being in love
have then a nobility in their natures more than is native
to them,—list me. The lieutenant to-night watches on the
court of guard: first, I must tell thee this—Desdemona is
235 directly in love with him.

RODERIGO

With him! why, 'tis not possible.

IAGO

Lay thy finger thus, and let thy soul be instructed. Mark me
with what violence she first loved the Moor, but for brag-
ging, and telling her fantastical lies: and will she love him
240 still for prating? Let not thy discreet heart think it. Her eye
must be fed; and what delight shall she have to look on the
devil? When the blood is made dull with the act of sport,
there should be,—again to inflame it and to give satiety
a fresh appetite,—loveliness in favour; sympathy in years,
245 manners, and beauties; all which the Moor is defective in:
now, for want of these required conveniences, her delicate
tenderness will find itself abused, begin to heave the gorge,
disrelish and abhor the Moor; very nature will instruct
her in it, and compel her to some second choice. Now
250 sir, this granted;—as it is a most pregnant and unforced
position,—who stands so eminently in the degree of this
fortune as Cassio does? a knave very voluble; no further
conscionable than in putting on the mere form of civil and
humane seeming, for the better compass of his salt and
255 most hidden loose affection? why, none; why, none;—a
slipper and subtle knave; a finder out of occasions; that has

an eye can stamp and counterfeit advantages, though true
advantage never present itself: a devilish knave! besides, the
knave is handsome, young, and hath all those requisites
260 in him that folly and green minds look after: a pestilent
complete knave; and the woman hath found him already.

RODERIGO

I cannot believe that in her; she is full of most blessed
condition.

IAGO

Blest fig's end! the wine she drinks is made of grapes: if she
265 had been blessed, she would never have loved the Moor:
blessed pudding! Didst thou not see her paddle with the
palm of his hand? didst not mark that?

RODERIGO

Yes, that I did; but that was but courtesy.

IAGO

Lechery, by this hand; an index and obscure prologue to
270 the history of lust and foul thoughts. They met so near
with their lips that their breaths embraced together. Villainous thoughts, Roderigo! when these mutualities so
marshal the way, hard at hand comes the master and main
exercise, the incorporate conclusion: pish!—But, sir, be
275 you ruled by me: I have brought you from Venice. Watch
you to-night: for the command, I'll lay't upon you: Cassio knows you not:—I'll not be far from you: do you find
some occasion to anger Cassio, either by speaking too
loud, or tainting his discipline, or from what other course
280 you please, which the time shall more favourably minister.

RODERIGO
Well.

IAGO
Sir, he is rash, and very sudden in choler, and haply with his truncheon may strike at you: provoke him, that he may; for even out of that will I cause these of Cyprus to mutiny,
285 whose qualification shall come into no true taste again but by the displanting of Cassio. So shall you have a shorter journey to your desires by the means I shall then have to prefer them; and the impediment most profitably removed, without the which there were no expectation of our prosperity.

RODERIGO
290 I will do this, if I can bring it to any opportunity.

IAGO
I warrant thee. Meet me by and by at the citadel: I must fetch his necessaries ashore. Farewell.

RODERIGO
Adieu.

[*Exit.*]

IAGO
That Cassio loves her, I do well believe it;
295 That she loves him, 'tis apt, and of great credit:
The Moor,—howbeit that I endure him not,—
Is of a constant, loving, noble nature;
And, I dare think, he'll prove to Desdemona
A most dear husband. Now, I do love her too;

300 Not out of absolute lust,—though, peradventure,
    I stand accountant for as great a sin,—
    But partly led to diet my revenge,
    For that I do suspect the lusty Moor
    Hath leap'd into my seat: the thought whereof
305 Doth, like a poisonous mineral, gnaw my inwards;
    And nothing can or shall content my soul
    Till I am even'd with him, wife for wife;
    Or, failing so, yet that I put the Moor
    At least into a jealousy so strong
310 That judgement cannot cure. Which thing to do,—
    If this poor trash of Venice, whom I trash
    For his quick hunting, stand the putting on,
    I'll have our Michael Cassio on the hip;
    Abuse him to the Moor in the rank garb,—
315 For I fear Cassio with my night-cap too;—
    Make the Moor thank me, love me, and reward me
    For making him egregiously an ass
    And practicing upon his peace and quiet
    Even to madness. 'Tis here, but yet confus'd:
320 Knavery's plain face is never seen till us'd.

[*Exit.*]

SCENE 2. A STREET.

[*Enter a* **HERALD** *with a proclamation;* **PEOPLE** *following.*]

HERALD
It is Othello's pleasure, our noble and valiant general, that
upon certain tidings now arrived, importing the mere
perdition of the Turkish fleet, every man put himself into

triumph; some to dance, some to make bonfires, each man
5   to what sport and revels his addiction leads him: for, besides
these beneficial news, it is the celebration of his nuptial:—
so much was his pleasure should be proclaimed. All offices
are open; and there is full liberty of feasting from this present hour of five till the bell have told eleven. Heaven bless
10   the isle of Cyprus and our noble general Othello!

[*Exeunt.*]

SCENE 3. A HALL IN THE CASTLE.

[*Enter* OTHELLO, DESDEMONA, CASSIO, *and* ATTENDANTS.]

OTHELLO
Good Michael, look you to the guard to-night:
Let's teach ourselves that honourable stop,
Not to out-sport discretion.

CASSIO
Iago hath direction what to do;
5   But, notwithstanding, with my personal eye
Will I look to't.

OTHELLO
Iago is most honest.
Michael, good night: to-morrow with your earliest
Let me have speech with you.—[*To* DESDEMONA.] Come,
10   my dear love,—
The purchase made, the fruits are to ensue;
That profit's yet to come 'tween me and you.—
Good-night.

[*Exeunt* OTHELLO, DESDEMONA, *and* ATTENDANTS.]

[*Enter* IAGO.]

CASSIO
Welcome, Iago; we must to the watch.

IAGO
15 Not this hour, lieutenant; 'tis not yet ten o' the clock. Our
general cast us thus early for the love of his Desdemona; who
let us not therefore blame: he hath not yet made wanton the
night with her; and she is sport for Jove.

CASSIO
She's a most exquisite lady.

IAGO
20 And, I'll warrant her, full of game.

CASSIO
Indeed, she is a most fresh and delicate creature.

IAGO
What an eye she has! methinks it sounds a parley to
provocation.

CASSIO
An inviting eye; and yet methinks right modest.

IAGO
25 And when she speaks, is it not an alarm to love?

Cassio

She is, indeed, perfection.

Iago

Well, happiness to their sheets! Come, lieutenant, I have a stoup of wine; and here without are a brace of Cyprus gallants that would fain have a measure to the health of black Othello.

Cassio

30 Not to-night, good Iago: I have very poor and unhappy brains for drinking: I could well wish courtesy would invent some other custom of entertainment.

Iago

O, they are our friends; but one cup: I'll drink for you.

Cassio

I have drunk but one cup to-night, and that was craftily
35 qualified too, and behold, what innovation it makes here: I am unfortunate in the infirmity, and dare not task my weakness with any more.

Iago

What, man! 'tis a night of revels: the gallants desire it.

Cassio

Where are they?

Iago

40 Here at the door; I pray you, call them in.

CASSIO

I'll do't; but it dislikes me.

[*Exit.*]

IAGO

If I can fasten but one cup upon him,
With that which he hath drunk to-night already,
He'll be as full of quarrel and offense
45 As my young mistress' dog. Now, my sick fool Roderigo,
Whom love hath turn'd almost the wrong side out,
To Desdemona hath to-night carous'd
Potations pottle-deep; and he's to watch:
Three lads of Cyprus,—noble swelling spirits,
50 That hold their honours in a wary distance,
The very elements of this warlike isle,—
Have I to-night fluster'd with flowing cups,
And they watch too. Now, 'mongst this flock of drunkards,
Am I to put our Cassio in some action
55 That may offend the isle:—but here they come:
If consequence do but approve my dream,
My boat sails freely, both with wind and stream.

[*Re-enter* CASSIO; *with him* MONTANO *and* GENTLEMEN; *followed by*
SERVANT *with wine.*]

CASSIO

'Fore heaven, they have given me a rouse already.

MONTANO

Good faith, a little one; not past a pint, as I am a soldier.

IAGO

60 Some wine, ho!

[*Sings.*]

"And let me the canakin clink, clink;
And let me the canakin clink.
A soldier's a man;
O, man's life's but a span;
65 Why then let a soldier drink."
Some wine, boys!

CASSIO

'Fore God, an excellent song.

IAGO

I learned it in England, where, indeed, they are most
potent in potting: your Dane, your German, and your
70 swag-bellied Hollander,—Drink, ho!—are nothing to
your English.

CASSIO

Is your Englishman so expert in his drinking?

IAGO

Why, he drinks you, with facility, your Dane dead drunk;
he sweats not to overthrow your Almain; he gives your
75 Hollander a vomit ere the next pottle can be filled.

CASSIO

To the health of our general!

MONTANO

I am for it, lieutenant; and I'll do you justice.

IAGO

O sweet England!

[*Sings.*]

"King Stephen was and a worthy peer,
80 His breeches cost him but a crown;
He held them sixpence all too dear,
With that he call'd the tailor lown.
"He was a wight of high renown,
And thou art but of low degree:
85 'Tis pride that pulls the country down;
Then take thine auld cloak about thee."
Some wine, ho!

CASSIO

Why, this is a more exquisite song than the other.

IAGO

Will you hear it again?

CASSIO

90 No; for I hold him to be unworthy of his place that does
those things.—Well,—God's above all, and there be souls
must be saved, and there be souls must not be saved.

IAGO

It's true, good lieutenant.

CASSIO

For mine own part,—no offence to the general, nor any
95 man of quality,—I hope to be saved.

IAGO

And so do I too, lieutenant.

CASSIO

Ay, but, by your leave, not before me; the lieutenant is to
be saved before the ancient. Let's have no more of this;
let's to our affairs.—Forgive us our sins!—Gentlemen,
100 let's look to our business. Do not think, gentlemen, I am
drunk: this is my ancient; this is my right hand, and this
is my left:—I am not drunk now; I can stand well enough,
and I speak well enough.

ALL

Excellent well.

CASSIO

105 Why, very well then: you must not think, then, that I am
drunk.

[Exit.]

MONTANO

To the platform, masters; come, let's set the watch.

IAGO

You see this fellow that is gone before;—
He is a soldier fit to stand by Caesar
110 And give direction: and do but see his vice;

'Tis to his virtue a just equinox,
The one as long as the other: 'tis pity of him.
I fear the trust Othello puts him in,
On some odd time of his infirmity,
115 Will shake this island.

MONTANO
But is he often thus?

IAGO
'Tis evermore the prologue to his sleep:
He'll watch the horologe a double set
If drink rock not his cradle.

MONTANO
120 It were well
The general were put in mind of it.
Perhaps he sees it not, or his good nature
Prizes the virtue that appears in Cassio,
And looks not on his evils: is not this true?

[*Enter* **RODERIGO**.]

IAGO
125 [*Aside to him.*] How now, Roderigo!
I pray you, after the lieutenant; go.

[*Exit* **RODERIGO**.]

MONTANO
And 'tis great pity that the noble Moor

Should hazard such a place as his own second
With one of an ingraft infirmity:
130 It were an honest action to say
So to the Moor.

IAGO
Not I, for this fair island;
I do love Cassio well; and would do much
To cure him of this evil.—But, hark! What noise?

[Cry within,—"Help! help!"]

[Re-enter CASSIO, driving in RODERIGO.]

CASSIO
135 You rogue! you rascal!

MONTANO
What's the matter, lieutenant?

CASSIO
A knave teach me my duty! I'll beat the knave into a twig-
gen bottle.

RODERIGO
Beat me!

CASSIO
140 Dost thou prate, rogue? *[Striking RODERIGO.]*

MONTANO
Nay, good lieutenant;

I pray you, sir, hold your hand.

CASSIO
Let me go, sir,
Or I'll knock you o'er the mazard.

MONTANO
145 Come, come, you're drunk.

CASSIO
Drunk!

[*They fight.*]

IAGO
[*Aside to* **RODERIGO**.] Away, I say! go out and cry a mutiny.

[*Exit* **RODERIGO**.]

Nay, good lieutenant,—alas,, gentlemen:—
Help, ho!—Lieutenant,—sir,—Montano,—sir:—
150 Help, masters!—Here's a goodly watch indeed!

[*Bell rings.*]

Who's that that rings the bell?—Diablo, ho!
The town will rise: God's will, lieutenant, hold;
You will be sham'd forever.

[*Re-enter* **OTHELLO** *and* **ATTENDANTS**.]

OTHELLO

What is the matter here?

MONTANO

155   Zounds, I bleed still; I am hurt to the death.

OTHELLO

Hold, for your lives!

IAGO

Hold, ho! lieutenant,—sir,—Montano,—gentlemen,—
Have you forgot all sense of place and duty?
Hold! the general speaks to you; hold, hold, for shame!

OTHELLO

160   Why, how now, ho! from whence ariseth this?
Are we turn'd Turks, and to ourselves do that
Which Heaven hath forbid the Ottomites?
For Christian shame, put by this barbarous brawl:
He that stirs next to carve for his own rage
165   Holds his soul light; he dies upon his motion.—
Silence that dreadful bell; it frights the isle
From her propriety.—What is the matter, masters?—
Honest Iago, that look'st dead with grieving,
Speak, who began this? on thy love, I charge thee.

IAGO

170   I do not know:—friends all but now, even now,
In quarter, and in terms like bride and groom
Devesting them for bed; and then, but now—
As if some planet had unwitted men,—
Swords out, and tilting one at other's breast

175 In opposition bloody. I cannot speak
Any beginning to this peevish odds;
And would in action glorious I had lost
Those legs that brought me to a part of it!

OTHELLO
How comes it, Michael, you are thus forgot?

CASSIO
180 I pray you, pardon me; I cannot speak.

OTHELLO
Worthy Montano, you were wont be civil;
The gravity and stillness of your youth
The world hath noted, and your name is great
In mouths of wisest censure: what's the matter,
185 That you unlace your reputation thus,
And spend your rich opinion for the name
Of a night-brawler? give me answer to it.

MONTANO
Worthy Othello, I am hurt to danger:
Your officer, Iago, can inform you,—
190 While I spare speech, which something now offends me,—
Of all that I do know: nor know I aught
By me that's said or done amiss this night:
Unless self-charity be sometimes a vice,
And to defend ourselves it be a sin
195 When violence assails us.

OTHELLO
Now, by heaven,

My blood begins my safer guides to rule;
And passion, having my best judgement collied,
Assays to lead the way. If I once stir,
200 Or do but lift this arm, the best of you
Shall sink in my rebuke. Give me to know
How this foul rout began, who set it on;
And he that is approv'd in this offense,
Though he had twinn'd with me, both at a birth,
205 Shall lose me.—What! in a town of war
Yet wild, the people's hearts brimful of fear,
To manage private and domestic quarrel,
In night, and on the court and guard of safety!
'Tis monstrous.—Iago, who began't?

MONTANO

210 If partially affin'd, or leagu'd in office,
Thou dost deliver more or less than truth,
Thou art no soldier.

IAGO

Touch me not so near:
I had rather have this tongue cut from my mouth
215 Than it should do offence to Michael Cassio;
Yet, I persuade myself, to speak the truth
Shall nothing wrong him.—Thus it is, general.
Montano and myself being in speech,
There comes a fellow crying out for help;
220 And Cassio following him with determin'd sword,
To execute upon him. Sir, this gentleman
Steps in to Cassio and entreats his pause:
Myself the crying fellow did pursue,
Lest by his clamour,—as it so fell out,—

225 The town might fall in fright: he, swift of foot,
Outran my purpose; and I return'd the rather
For that I heard the clink and fall of swords,
And Cassio high in oath; which till to-night
I ne'er might say before. When I came back,—
230 For this was brief,—I found them close together,
At blow and thrust; even as again they were
When you yourself did part them.
More of this matter cannot I report;—
But men are men; the best sometimes forget:—
235 Though Cassio did some little wrong to him,—
As men in rage strike those that wish them best,—
Yet surely Cassio, I believe, receiv'd
From him that fled some strange indignity,
Which patience could not pass.

OTHELLO
240 I know, Iago,
Thy honesty and love doth mince this matter,
Making it light to Cassio. Cassio, I love thee;
But never more be officer of mine.—

[*Re-enter* **DESDEMONA**, *attended.*]

Look, if my gentle love be not rais'd up!—
245 I'll make thee an example.

DESDEMONA
What's the matter?

OTHELLO
All's well now, sweeting; come away to bed.

[*To* **Montano**, *who is led off.*]

Sir, for your hurts, myself will be your surgeon:
Lead him off.
250 Iago, look with care about the town,
And silence those whom this vile brawl distracted.—
Come, Desdemona: 'tis the soldiers' life
To have their balmy slumbers wak'd with strife.

[*Exeunt all but* **Iago** *and* **Cassio.**]

Iago
What, are you hurt, lieutenant?

Cassio
255 Ay, past all surgery.

Iago
Marry, heaven forbid!

Cassio
Reputation, reputation, reputation! O, I have lost my reputation! I have lost the immortal part of myself, and what
remains is bestial.—My reputation, Iago, my reputation!

Iago
260 As I am an honest man, I thought you had received some
bodily wound; there is more sense in that than in reputation.
Reputation is an idle and most false imposition; oft got without merit and lost without deserving: you have lost no reputation at all, unless you repute yourself such a loser. What, man!
265 there are ways to recover the general again: you are but now

cast in his mood, a punishment more in policy than in malice; even so as one would beat his offenceless dog to affright an imperious lion: sue to him again, and he is yours.

CASSIO

270 I will rather sue to be despised than to deceive so good a commander with so slight, so drunken, and so indiscreet an officer. Drunk? and speak parrot? and squabble? swagger? swear? and discourse fustian with one's own shadow?—O thou invisible spirit of wine, if thou hast no name to be known by, let us call thee devil!

IAGO

275 What was he that you followed with your sword? What had he done to you?

CASSIO

I know not.

IAGO

Is't possible?

CASSIO

I remember a mass of things, but nothing distinctly; a
280 quarrel, but nothing wherefore.—O God, that men should put an enemy in their mouths to steal away their brains! that we should, with joy, pleasance, revel, and applause, transform ourselves into beasts!

IAGO

Why, but you are now well enough: how came you thus
285 recovered?

CASSIO

It hath pleased the devil drunkenness to give place to the
devil wrath: one unperfectness shows me another, to make
me frankly despise myself.

IAGO

Come, you are too severe a moraler: as the time, the place,
290 and the condition of this country stands, I could heartily
wish this had not befallen; but since it is as it is, mend it
for your own good.

CASSIO

I will ask him for my place again;—he shall tell me I am
a drunkard! Had I as many mouths as Hydra, such an
295 answer would stop them all. To be now a sensible man,
by and by a fool, and presently a beast! O strange!—Every
inordinate cup is unbless'd, and the ingredient is a devil.

IAGO

Come, come, good wine is a good familiar creature, if it be
well used: exclaim no more against it. And, good lieuten-
300 ant, I think you think I love you.

CASSIO

I have well approved it, sir.—I drunk!

IAGO

You, or any man living, may be drunk at a time, man. I'll
tell you what you shall do. Our general's wife is now the
general;—I may say so in this respect, for that he hath
305 devoted and given up himself to the contemplation, mark,
and denotement of her parts and graces:—confess yourself

freely to her; importune her help to put you in your place again: she is of so free, so kind, so apt, so blessed a disposition, she holds it a vice in her goodness not to do
310 more than she is requested: this broken joint between you and her husband entreat her to splinter; and, my fortunes against any lay worth naming, this crack of your love shall grow stronger than it was before.

CASSIO
You advise me well.

IAGO
315 I protest, in the sincerity of love and honest kindness.

CASSIO
I think it freely; and betimes in the morning I will beseech the virtuous Desdemona to undertake for me; I am desperate of my fortunes if they check me here.

IAGO
You are in the right. Good-night, lieutenant; I must to
320 the watch.

CASSIO
Good night, honest Iago.

[*Exit.*]

IAGO
And what's he, then, that says I play the villain?
When this advice is free I give and honest,
Probal to thinking, and, indeed, the course

325   To win the Moor again? For 'tis most easy
The inclining Desdemona to subdue
In any honest suit: she's fram'd as fruitful
As the free elements. And then for her
To win the Moor,—were't to renounce his baptism,
330   All seals and symbols of redeemèd sin,—
His soul is so enfetter'd to her love
That she may make, unmake, do what she list,
Even as her appetite shall play the god
With his weak function. How am I, then, a villain
335   To counsel Cassio to this parallel course,
Directly to his good? Divinity of hell!
When devils will the blackest sins put on,
They do suggest at first with heavenly shows,
As I do now: for whiles this honest fool
340   Plies Desdemona to repair his fortune,
And she for him pleads strongly to the Moor,
I'll pour this pestilence into his ear,—
That she repeals him for her body's lust;
And by how much she strives to do him good,
345   She shall undo her credit with the Moor.
So will I turn her virtue into pitch;
And out of her own goodness make the net
That shall enmesh them all.

[*Enter* **RODERIGO.**]

How now, Roderigo!

RODERIGO

350   I do follow here in the chase, not like a hound that hunts,
but one that fills up the cry. My money is almost spent; I

have been to-night exceedingly well cudgelled; and I think
the issue will be—I shall have so much experience for my
pains: and so, with no money at all and a little more wit,
355 return again to Venice.

IAGO
How poor are they that have not patience!
What wound did ever heal but by degrees?
Thou know'st we work by wit, and not by witchcraft;
And wit depends on dilatory time.
360 Does't not go well? Cassio hath beaten thee,
And thou, by that small hurt, hast cashier'd Cassio;
Though other things grow fair against the sun,
Yet fruits that blossom first will first be ripe:
Content thyself awhile.—By the mass, 'tis morning;
365 Pleasure and action make the hours seem short.—
Retire thee; go where thou art billeted:
Away, I say; thou shalt know more hereafter;
Nay, get thee gone.

[*Exit* **RODERIGO**.]

Two things are to be done,—
370 My wife must move for Cassio to her mistress;
I'll set her on;
Myself the while to draw the Moor apart,
And bring him jump when he may Cassio find
Soliciting his wife. Ay, that's the way;
375 Dull not device by coldness and delay.

[*Exit.*]

ACT 3.

Scene 1. Cyprus. Before the Castle.

[Enter Cassio *and some* Musicians.]

Cassio
Masters, play here,—I will content your pains,
Something that's brief; and bid "Good-morrow, general."

[Music.]

[Enter Clown.]

Clown
Why, masters, have your instruments been in Naples, that
they speak i' the nose thus?

First musician
5 How, sir, how!

Clown
Are these, I pray you, wind instruments?

First musician
Ay, marry, are they, sir.

CLOWN

O, thereby hangs a tale.

FIRST MUSICIAN

Whereby hangs a tale, sir?

CLOWN

10 Marry, sir, by many a wind instrument that I know. But, masters, here's money for you: and the general so likes your music, that he desires you, for love's sake, to make no more noise with it.

FIRST MUSICIAN

Well, sir, we will not.

CLOWN

15 If you have any music that may not be heard, to't again: but, as they say, to hear music the general does not greatly care.

FIRST MUSICIAN

We have none such, sir.

CLOWN

Then put up your pipes in your bag, for I'll away: go, vanish into air, away!

[*Exeunt* MUSICIANS.]

CASSIO

20 Dost thou hear, mine honest friend?

Clown

No, I hear not your honest friend; I hear you.

Cassio

Pr'ythee, keep up thy quillets. There's a poor piece of gold for thee: if the gentlewoman that attends the general's wife be stirring, tell her there's one Cassio entreats her a little
25 favour of speech: wilt thou do this?

Clown

She is stirring, sir; if she will stir hither I shall seem to notify unto her.

Cassio

Do, good my friend.

[*Exit* **Clown.**]

[*Enter* **Iago.**]

In happy time, Iago.

Iago

30 You have not been a-bed, then?

Cassio

Why, no; the day had broke
Before we parted. I have made bold, Iago,
To send in to your wife: my suit to her
Is, that she will to virtuous Desdemona
35 Procure me some access.

IAGO

I'll send her to you presently;
And I'll devise a mean to draw the Moor
Out of the way, that your converse and business
May be more free.

CASSIO

40 I humbly thank you for't.

[*Exit* IAGO.]

I never knew
A Florentine more kind and honest.

[*Enter* EMILIA.]

EMILIA

Good-morrow, good lieutenant; I am sorry
For your displeasure; but all will sure be well.
45 The general and his wife are talking of it;
And she speaks for you stoutly: the Moor replies
That he you hurt is of great fame in Cyprus
And great affinity, and that, in wholesome wisdom,
He might not but refuse you; but he protests he loves you
50 And needs no other suitor but his likings
To take the safest occasion by the front
To bring you in again.

CASSIO

Yet, I beseech you,—
If you think fit, or that it may be done,—
55 Give me advantage of some brief discourse

With Desdemona alone.

EMILIA
Pray you, come in:
I will bestow you where you shall have time
To speak your bosom freely.

CASSIO
60 I am much bound to you.

[*Exeunt.*]

SCENE 2. CYPRUS. A ROOM IN THE CASTLE.

[*Enter* **OTHELLO, IAGO,** *and* **GENTLEMEN.**]

OTHELLO
These letters give, Iago, to the pilot;
And by him do my duties to the senate:
That done, I will be walking on the works;
Repair there to me.

IAGO
5 Well, my good lord, I'll do't.

OTHELLO
This fortification, gentlemen,—shall we see't?

GENTLEMEN
We'll wait upon your lordship.

[*Exeunt.*]

Scene 3. Cyprus. The Garden of the Castle.

[*Enter* **Desdemona**, **Cassio**, *and* **Emilia**.]

Desdemona

Be thou assured, good Cassio, I will do
All my abilities in thy behalf.

Emilia

Good madam, do: I warrant it grieves my husband
As if the cause were his.

Desdemona

5 O, that's an honest fellow.—Do not doubt, Cassio,
But I will have my lord and you again
As friendly as you were.

Cassio

Bounteous madam,
Whatever shall become of Michael Cassio,
10 He's never anything but your true servant.

Desdemona

I know't,—I thank you. You do love my lord:
You have known him long; and be you well assur'd
He shall in strangeness stand no farther off
Than in a politic distance.

Cassio

15 Ay, but, lady,
That policy may either last so long,
Or feed upon such nice and waterish diet,

Or breed itself so out of circumstance,
That, I being absent, and my place supplied,
20 My general will forget my love and service.

DESDEMONA
Do not doubt that; before Emilia here
I give thee warrant of thy place: assure thee,
If I do vow a friendship, I'll perform it
To the last article: my lord shall never rest;
25 I'll watch him tame, and talk him out of patience;
His bed shall seem a school, his board a shrift;
I'll intermingle everything he does
With Cassio's suit: therefore be merry, Cassio;
For thy solicitor shall rather die
30 Than give thy cause away.

EMILIA
Madam, here comes my lord.

CASSIO
Madam, I'll take my leave.

DESDEMONA
Why, stay, and hear me speak.

CASSIO
Madam, not now. I am very ill at ease,
35 Unfit for mine own purposes.

DESDEMONA
Well, do your discretion.

[*Exit* CASSIO.]

[*Enter* OTHELLO *and* IAGO.]

IAGO
Ha! I like not that.

OTHELLO
What dost thou say?

IAGO
Nothing, my lord: or if—I know not what.

OTHELLO
40 Was not that Cassio parted from my wife?

IAGO
Cassio, my lord! No, sure, I cannot think it,
That he would steal away so guilty-like,
Seeing you coming.

OTHELLO
I do believe 'twas he.

DESDEMONA
45 How now, my lord!
I have been talking with a suitor here,
A man that languishes in your displeasure.

OTHELLO
Who is't you mean?

DESDEMONA

Why, your lieutenant, Cassio. Good my lord,
50 If I have any grace or power to move you,
His present reconciliation take;
For if he be not one that truly loves you,
That errs in ignorance and not in cunning,
I have no judgement in an honest face:
55 I pr'ythee, call him back.

OTHELLO

Went he hence now?

DESDEMONA

Ay, sooth; so humbled
That he hath left part of his grief with me
To suffer with him. Good love, call him back.

OTHELLO

60 Not now, sweet Desdemon; some other time.

DESDEMONA

But shall't be shortly?

OTHELLO

The sooner, sweet, for you.

DESDEMONA

Shall't be to-night at supper?

OTHELLO

No, not to-night.

DESDEMONA

65 To-morrow dinner then?

OTHELLO

I shall not dine at home;
I meet the captains at the citadel.

DESDEMONA

Why then to-morrow night; or Tuesday morn;
On Tuesday noon, or night; on Wednesday morn:—
70 I pr'ythee, name the time; but let it not
Exceed three days: in faith, he's penitent;
And yet his trespass, in our common reason,—
Save that, they say, the wars must make examples
Out of their best,—is not almost a fault
75 To incur a private check. When shall he come?
Tell me, Othello: I wonder in my soul,
What you would ask me, that I should deny,
Or stand so mammering on. What! Michael Cassio,
That came awooing with you; and so many a time,
80 When I have spoke of you dispraisingly,
Hath ta'en your part;—to have so much to do
To bring him in! Trust me, I could do much,—

OTHELLO

Pr'ythee, no more; let him come when he will;
I will deny thee nothing.

DESDEMONA

85 Why, this is not a boon;
'Tis as I should entreat you wear your gloves,
Or feed on nourishing dishes, or keep you warm,

Or sue to you to do a peculiar profit
To your own person: nay, when I have a suit
90 Wherein I mean to touch your love indeed,
It shall be full of poise and difficult weight,
And fearful to be granted.

OTHELLO

I will deny thee nothing:
Whereon, I do beseech thee, grant me this,
95 To leave me but a little to myself.

DESDEMONA

Shall I deny you? no: farewell, my lord.

OTHELLO

Farewell, my Desdemona: I'll come to thee straight.

DESDEMONA

Emilia, come.—Be as your fancies teach you;
Whate'er you be, I am obedient.

[*Exit with* **EMILIA**.]

OTHELLO

100 Excellent wretch! Perdition catch my soul,
But I do love thee! and when I love thee not,
Chaos is come again.

IAGO

My noble lord,—

OTHELLO
What dost thou say, Iago?

IAGO
105 Did Michael Cassio, when you woo'd my lady,
Know of your love?

OTHELLO
He did, from first to last: why dost thou ask?

IAGO
But for a satisfaction of my thought;
No further harm.

OTHELLO
110 Why of thy thought, Iago?

IAGO
I did not think he had been acquainted with her.

OTHELLO
O, yes; and went between us very oft.

IAGO
Indeed!

OTHELLO
Indeed! ay, indeed:—discern'st thou aught in that?
115 Is he not honest?

IAGO
Honest, my lord!

OTHELLO

Honest! ay, honest.

IAGO

My lord, for aught I know.

OTHELLO

What dost thou think?

IAGO

120 Think, my lord!

OTHELLO

Think, my lord! By heaven, he echoes me,
As if there were some monster in his thought
Too hideous to be shown.—Thou dost mean something:
I heard thee say even now,—thou lik'dst not that,
125 When Cassio left my wife. What didst not like?
And when I told thee he was of my counsel
In my whole course of wooing, thou criedst, "Indeed!"
And didst contract and purse thy brow together,
As if thou then hadst shut up in thy brain
130 Some horrible conceit: if thou dost love me,
Show me thy thought.

IAGO

My lord, you know I love you.

OTHELLO

I think thou dost;
And,—for I know thou'rt full of love and honesty
135 And weigh'st thy words before thou giv'st them breath,—

Therefore these stops of thine fright me the more:
For such things in a false disloyal knave
Are tricks of custom; but in a man that's just
They're close delations, working from the heart,
140   That passion cannot rule.

IAGO
For Michael Cassio,
I dare be sworn I think that he is honest.

OTHELLO
I think so too.

IAGO
Men should be what they seem;
145   Or those that be not, would they might seem none!

OTHELLO
Certain, men should be what they seem.

IAGO
Why, then, I think Cassio's an honest man.

OTHELLO
Nay, yet there's more in this:
I pr'ythee, speak to me as to thy thinkings,
150   As thou dost ruminate; and give thy worst of thoughts
The worst of words.

IAGO
Good my lord, pardon me:
Though I am bound to every act of duty,

I am not bound to that all slaves are free to.
155   Utter my thoughts? Why, say they are vile and false;—
As where's that palace whereinto foul things
Sometimes intrude not? who has a breast so pure
But some uncleanly apprehensions
Keep leets and law-days, and in session sit
160   With meditations lawful?

OTHELLO
Thou dost conspire against thy friend, Iago,
If thou but think'st him wrong'd and mak'st his ear
A stranger to thy thoughts.

IAGO
I do beseech you,—
165   Though I perchance am vicious in my guess,
As, I confess, it is my nature's plague
To spy into abuses, and of my jealousy
Shape faults that are not,—that your wisdom yet,
From one that so imperfectly conceits,
170   Would take no notice; nor build yourself a trouble
Out of his scattering and unsure observance:—
It were not for your quiet nor your good,
Nor for my manhood, honesty, or wisdom,
To let you know my thoughts.

OTHELLO
175   What dost thou mean?

IAGO
Good name in man and woman, dear my lord,
Is the immediate jewel of their souls:

Who steals my purse steals trash; 'tis something, nothing;
'Twas mine, 'tis his, and has been slave to thousands;
180 But he that filches from me my good name
Robs me of that which not enriches him
And makes me poor indeed.

OTHELLO
By heaven, I'll know thy thoughts.

IAGO
You cannot, if my heart were in your hand;
185 Nor shall not, whilst 'tis in my custody.

OTHELLO
Ha!

IAGO
O, beware, my lord, of jealousy;
It is the green-ey'd monster which doth mock
The meat it feeds on: that cuckold lives in bliss
190 Who, certain of his fate, loves not his wronger;
But O, what damnèd minutes tells he o'er
Who dotes, yet doubts, suspects, yet strongly loves!

OTHELLO
O misery!

IAGO
Poor and content is rich, and rich enough;
195 But riches fineless is as poor as winter
To him that ever fears he shall be poor;—
Good heaven, the souls of all my tribe defend

From jealousy!

OTHELLO
Why, why is this?
200 Think'st thou I'd make a life of jealousy,
To follow still the changes of the moon
With fresh suspicions? No; to be once in doubt
Is once to be resolv'd: exchange me for a goat
When I shall turn the business of my soul
205 To such exsufflicate and blown surmises,
Matching thy inference. 'Tis not to make me jealous,
To say my wife is fair, feeds well, loves company,
Is free of speech, sings, plays, and dances well;
Where virtue is, these are more virtuous:
210 Nor from mine own weak merits will I draw
The smallest fear or doubt of her revolt;
For she had eyes and chose me. No, Iago;
I'll see before I doubt; when I doubt, prove;
And on the proof, there is no more but this,—
215 Away at once with love or jealousy!

IAGO
I am glad of it; for now I shall have reason
To show the love and duty that I bear you
With franker spirit: therefore, as I am bound,
Receive it from me:—I speak not yet of proof.
220 Look to your wife; observe her well with Cassio;
Wear your eye thus, not jealous nor secure:
I would not have your free and noble nature,
Out of self-bounty, be abus'd; look to't.
I know our country disposition well;
225 In Venice they do let heaven see the pranks

They dare not show their husbands; their best conscience
Is not to leave undone, but keep unknown.

OTHELLO
Dost thou say so?

IAGO
She did deceive her father, marrying you;
230 And when she seem'd to shake and fear your looks,
She loved them most.

OTHELLO
And so she did.

IAGO
Why, go to then;
She that, so young, could give out such a seeming,
235 To seal her father's eyes up close as oak,—
He thought 'twas witchcraft,—but I am much to blame;
I humbly do beseech you of your pardon
For too much loving you.

OTHELLO
I am bound to thee for ever.

IAGO
240 I see this hath a little dash'd your spirits.

OTHELLO
Not a jot, not a jot.

IAGO

Trust me, I fear it has.

I hope you will consider what is spoke

Comes from my love; but I do see you're mov'd:—

245 I am to pray you not to strain my speech

To grosser issues nor to larger reach

Than to suspicion.

OTHELLO

I will not.

IAGO

Should you do so, my lord,

250 My speech should fall into such vile success

Which my thoughts aim'd not. Cassio's my worthy friend:—

My lord, I see you're mov'd.

OTHELLO

No, not much mov'd.

255 I do not think but Desdemona's honest.

IAGO

Long live she so! and long live you to think so!

OTHELLO

And yet, how nature erring from itself,—

IAGO

Ay, there's the point:—as,—to be bold with you,—

Not to affect many proposed matches,

260 Of her own clime, complexion, and degree,

Whereto we see in all things nature tends,—
Foh! one may smell in such a will most rank,
Foul disproportion, thoughts unnatural:—
But pardon me: I do not in position
265 Distinctly speak of her; though I may fear,
Her will, recoiling to her better judgement,
May fall to match you with her country forms,
And happily repent.

OTHELLO

Farewell, farewell:
270 If more thou dost perceive, let me know more;
Set on thy wife to observe: leave me, Iago.

IAGO

[*Going.*] My lord, I take my leave.

OTHELLO

Why did I marry?—This honest creature doubtless
Sees and knows more, much more, than he unfolds.

IAGO

275 [*Returning.*] My lord, I would I might entreat your honour
To scan this thing no further; leave it to time:
Though it be fit that Cassio have his place,—
For sure he fills it up with great ability,—
Yet, if you please to hold him off awhile,
280 You shall by that perceive him and his means:
Note if your lady strain his entertainment
With any strong or vehement importunity;
Much will be seen in that. In the meantime,

Let me be thought too busy in my fears,—
285 As worthy cause I have to fear I am,—
And hold her free, I do beseech your honour.

OTHELLO

Fear not my government.

IAGO

I once more take my leave.

[*Exit.*]

OTHELLO

This fellow's of exceeding honesty,
290 And knows all qualities, with a learned spirit,
Of human dealings. If I do prove her haggard,
Though that her jesses were my dear heartstrings,
I'd whistle her off, and let her down the wind
To prey at fortune. Haply, for I am black,
295 And have not those soft parts of conversation
That chamberers have; or for I am declin'd
Into the vale of years,—yet that's not much,—
She's gone; I am abus'd, and my relief
Must be to loathe her. O curse of marriage,
300 That we can call these delicate creatures ours,
And not their appetites! I had rather be a toad,
And live upon the vapor of a dungeon,
Than keep a corner in the thing I love
For others' uses. Yet, 'tis the plague of great ones:
305 Prerogativ'd are they less than the base;
'Tis destiny unshunnable, like death:

Even then this forkèd plague is fated to us
When we do quicken. Desdemona comes:
If she be false, O, then heaven mocks itself!—
310   I'll not believe't.

[*Re-enter* **DESDEMONA** *and* **EMILIA.**]

DESDEMONA
How now, my dear Othello!
Your dinner, and the generous islanders
By you invited, do attend your presence.

OTHELLO
I am to blame.

DESDEMONA
315   Why do you speak so faintly?
Are you not well?

OTHELLO
I have a pain upon my forehead here.

DESDEMONA
Faith, that's with watching; 'twill away again;
Let me but bind it hard, within this hour
320   It will be well.

OTHELLO
Your napkin is too little;

[*He puts the handkerchief from him, and she drops it.*]

Let it alone. Come, I'll go in with you.

DESDEMONA
I am very sorry that you are not well.

[*Exeunt* **OTHELLO** *and* **DESDEMONA**.]

EMILIA
I am glad I have found this napkin;
325 This was her first remembrance from the Moor.
My wayward husband hath a hundred times
Woo'd me to steal it; but she so loves the token,—
For he conjur'd her she should ever keep it,—
That she reserves it evermore about her
330 To kiss and talk to. I'll have the work ta'en out,
And give't Iago:
What he will do with it heaven knows, not I;
I nothing but to please his fantasy.

[*Re-enter* **IAGO**.]

IAGO
How now! what do you here alone?

EMILIA
335 Do not you chide; I have a thing for you.

IAGO
A thing for me!—it is a common thing.

EMILIA
Ha!

IAGO

To have a foolish wife.

EMILIA

O, is that all? What will you give me now
340 For that same handkerchief?

IAGO

What handkerchief?

EMILIA

What handkerchief!
Why, that the Moor first gave to Desdemona;
That which so often you did bid me steal.

IAGO

345 Hast stol'n it from her?

EMILIA

No, faith; she let it drop by negligence,
And, to the advantage, I being here, took't up.
Look, here it is.

IAGO

A good wench; give it me.

EMILIA

350 What will you do with't, that you have been so earnest
To have me filch it?

IAGO

[*Snatching it.*] Why, what's that to you?

EMILIA

If it be not for some purpose of import,
Give't me again: poor lady, she'll run mad
355　When she shall lack it.

IAGO

Be not acknown on't; I have use for it.
Go, leave me.

[*Exit* **EMILIA**.]

I will in Cassio's lodging lose this napkin,
And let him find it. Trifles light as air
360　Are to the jealous confirmations strong
As proofs of holy writ: this may do something.
The Moor already changes with my poison:
Dangerous conceits are in their natures poisons,
Which at the first are scarce found to distaste,
365　But, with a little act upon the blood,
Burn like the mines of sulphur.—I did say so:—
Look, where he comes!
Not poppy, nor mandragora,
Nor all the drowsy syrups of the world,
370　Shall ever medicine thee to that sweet sleep
Which thou ow'dst yesterday.

[*Re-enter* **OTHELLO**.]

OTHELLO

Ha! ha! false to me?

IAGO

Why, how now, general! no more of that.

OTHELLO

Avaunt! be gone! thou hast set me on the rack:—
375 I swear 'tis better to be much abus'd
Than but to know't a little.

IAGO

How now, my lord!

OTHELLO

What sense had I of her stol'n hours of lust?
I saw't not, thought it not, it harm'd not me:
380 I slept the next night well, was free and merry;
I found not Cassio's kisses on her lips:
He that is robb'd, not wanting what is stol'n,
Let him not know't and he's not robb'd at all.

IAGO

I am sorry to hear this.

OTHELLO

385 I had been happy if the general camp,
Pioners and all, had tasted her sweet body,
So I had nothing known. O, now, for ever
Farewell the tranquil mind! farewell content!
Farewell the plumèd troop and the big wars
390 That make ambition virtue! O, farewell,
Farewell the neighing steed and the shrill trump,
The spirit-stirring drum, the ear-piercing fife,
The royal banner, and all quality,

Pride, pomp, and circumstance of glorious war!
395 And, O you mortal engines, whose rude throats
The immortal Jove's dread clamors counterfeit,
Farewell! Othello's occupation's gone!

IAGO

Is't possible, my lord?—

OTHELLO

Villain, be sure thou prove my love a whore;—
400 [*Taking him by the throat.*] Be sure of it. Give me the ocular
proof;
Or, by the worth of man's eternal soul,
Thou hadst been better have been born a dog
Than answer my wak'd wrath!

IAGO

405 Is't come to this?

OTHELLO

Make me to see't; or at the least so prove it,
That the probation bear no hinge nor loop
To hang a doubt on; or woe upon thy life!

IAGO

My noble lord,—

OTHELLO

410 If thou dost slander her and torture me,
Never pray more; abandon all remorse;
On horror's head horrors accumulate;
Do deeds to make heaven weep, all earth amaz'd;

For nothing canst thou to damnation add
415   Greater than that.

IAGO

O grace! O heaven defend me!
Are you a man? have you a soul or sense?—
God be wi' you; take mine office.—O wretched fool,
That liv'st to make thine honesty a vice!—
420   O monstrous world! Take note, take note, O world,
To be direct and honest is not safe.—
I thank you for this profit; and from hence
I'll love no friend, sith love breeds such offense.

OTHELLO

Nay, stay:—thou shouldst be honest.

IAGO

425   I should be wise; for honesty's a fool,
And loses that it works for.

OTHELLO

By the world,
I think my wife be honest, and think she is not;
I think that thou art just, and think thou art not:
430   I'll have some proof: her name, that was as fresh
As Dian's visage, is now begrim'd and black
As mine own face.—If there be cords or knives,
Poison or fire, or suffocating streams,
I'll not endure 't.—Would I were satisfied!

IAGO

435   I see, sir, you are eaten up with passion:

I do repent me that I put it to you.
You would be satisfied?

OTHELLO
Would! nay, I will.

IAGO
And may: but how? how satisfied, my lord?
440 Would you, the supervisor, grossly gape on,—
Behold her tupp'd?

OTHELLO
Death and damnation! O!

IAGO
It were a tedious difficulty, I think,
To bring them to that prospect: damn them then,
445 If ever mortal eyes do see them bolster
More than their own! What then? how then?
What shall I say? Where's satisfaction?
It is impossible you should see this
Were they as prime as goats, as hot as monkeys,
450 As salt as wolves in pride, and fools as gross
As ignorance made drunk. But yet, I say,
If imputation and strong circumstances,—
Which lead directly to the door of truth,—
Will give you satisfaction, you may have't.

OTHELLO
455 Give me a living reason she's disloyal.

IAGO

I do not like the office;
But, sith I am enter'd in this cause so far,—
Prick'd to it by foolish honesty and love,—
I will go on. I lay with Cassio lately;
460 And, being troubled with a raging tooth,
I could not sleep.
There are a kind of men so loose of soul,
That in their sleeps will mutter their affairs:
One of this kind is Cassio:
465 In sleep I heard him say, "Sweet Desdemona,
Let us be wary, let us hide our loves";
And then, sir, would he gripe and wring my hand,
Cry, "O sweet creature!" and then kiss me hard,
As if he pluck'd up kisses by the roots,
470 That grew upon my lips: then laid his leg
Over my thigh, and sigh'd and kiss'd; and then
Cried, "Cursed fate that gave thee to the Moor!"

OTHELLO

O monstrous! monstrous!

IAGO

Nay, this was but his dream.

OTHELLO

475 But this denoted a foregone conclusion:
'Tis a shrewd doubt, though it be but a dream.

IAGO

And this may help to thicken other proofs
That do demónstrate thinly.

OTHELLO

I'll tear her all to pieces.

IAGO

480 Nay, but be wise: yet we see nothing done;
She may be honest yet. Tell me but this,—
Have you not sometimes seen a handkerchief
Spotted with strawberries in your wife's hand?

OTHELLO

I gave her such a one; 'twas my first gift.

IAGO

485 I know not that: but such a handkerchief,—
I am sure it was your wife's,—did I today
See Cassio wipe his beard with.

OTHELLO

If it be that,—

IAGO

If it be that, or any that was hers,
490 It speaks against her with the other proofs.

OTHELLO

O, that the slave had forty thousand lives,—
One is too poor, too weak for my revenge!
Now do I see 'tis true.—Look here, Iago;
All my fond love thus do I blow to heaven:
495 'Tis gone.—
Arise, black vengeance, from thy hollow hell!
Yield up, O love, thy crown and hearted throne

To tyrannous hate! swell, bosom, with thy fraught,
For 'tis of aspics' tongues!

IAGO

500   Yet be content.

OTHELLO

O, blood, Iago, blood!

IAGO

Patience, I say; your mind perhaps may change.

OTHELLO

Never, Iago. Like to the Pontic Sea,
Whose icy current and compulsive course
505   Ne'er feels retiring ebb, but keeps due on
To the Propontic and the Hellespont;
Even so my bloody thoughts, with violent pace,
Shall ne'er look back, ne'er ebb to humble love,
Till that a capable and wide revenge
510   Swallow them up.—Now, by yond marble heaven,
In the due reverence of a sacred vow [*Kneels.*]
I here engage my words.

IAGO

Do not rise yet.—[*Kneels.*]
Witness, you ever-burning lights above,
515   You elements that clip us round about,—
Witness that here Iago doth give up
The execution of his wit, hands, heart,
To wrong'd Othello's service! Let him command,
And to obey shall be in me remorse,

520　What bloody business ever.

[*They rise.*]

OTHELLO
I greet thy love,
Not with vain thanks, but with acceptance bounteous,
And will upon the instant put thee to't:
Within these three days let me hear thee say
525　That Cassio's not alive.

IAGO
My friend is dead; 'tis done at your request:
But let her live.

OTHELLO
Damn her, lewd minx! O, damn her!
Come, go with me apart; I will withdraw
530　To furnish me with some swift means of death
For the fair devil. Now art thou my lieutenant.

IAGO
I am your own for ever.

[*Exeunt.*]

SCENE 4. CYPRUS. BEFORE THE CASTLE.

[*Enter* DESDEMONA, EMILIA, *and* CLOWN.]

DESDEMONA
Do you know, sirrah, where Lieutenant Cassio lies?

CLOWN

I dare not say he lies anywhere.

DESDEMONA

Why, man?

CLOWN

He's a soldier; and for one to say a soldier lies is stabbing.

DESDEMONA

5   Go to: where lodges he?

CLOWN

To tell you where he lodges is to tell you where I lie.

DESDEMONA

Can anything be made of this?

CLOWN

I know not where he lodges; and for me to devise a lodging, and say he lies here or he lies there were to lie in mine
10   own throat.

DESDEMONA

Can you inquire him out, and be edified by report?

CLOWN

I will catechize the world for him; that is, make questions
and by them answer.

DESDEMONA

Seek him, bid him come hither: tell him I have moved my
15 lord on his behalf, and hope all will be well.

CLOWN

To do this is within the compass of man's wit; and therefore I will attempt the doing it.

[*Exit.*]

DESDEMONA

Where should I lose that handkerchief, Emilia?

EMILIA

I know not, madam.

DESDEMONA

20 Believe me, I had rather have lost my purse
Full of crusadoes: and, but my noble Moor
Is true of mind and made of no such baseness
As jealous creatures are, it were enough
To put him to ill thinking.

EMILIA

25 Is he not jealous?

DESDEMONA

Who, he? I think the sun where he was born
Drew all such humours from him.

EMILIA

Look, where he comes.

DESDEMONA
I will not leave him now till Cassio
30   Be call'd to him.

[*Enter* **OTHELLO**.]

How is't with you, my lord?

OTHELLO
Well, my good lady.— [*Aside.*] O, hardness to dissemble!—
How do you, Desdemona?

DESDEMONA
Well, my good lord.

OTHELLO
35   Give me your hand: this hand is moist, my lady.

DESDEMONA
It yet hath felt no age nor known no sorrow.

OTHELLO
This argues fruitfulness and liberal heart:—
Hot, hot, and moist: this hand of yours requires
A sequester from liberty, fasting, and prayer,
40   Much castigation, exercise devout;
For here's a young and sweating devil here
That commonly rebels. 'Tis a good hand,
A frank one.

DESDEMONA
You may, indeed, say so;

45 For 'twas that hand that gave away my heart.

OTHELLO
A liberal hand: the hearts of old gave hands;
But our new heraldry is hands, not hearts.

DESDEMONA
I cannot speak of this. Come now, your promise.

OTHELLO
What promise, chuck?

DESDEMONA
50 I have sent to bid Cassio come speak with you.

OTHELLO
I have a salt and sorry rheum offends me;
Lend me thy handkerchief.

DESDEMONA
Here, my lord.

OTHELLO
That which I gave you.

DESDEMONA
55 I have it not about me.

OTHELLO
Not?

DESDEMONA

No, faith, my lord.

OTHELLO

That is a fault. That handkerchief
Did an Egyptian to my mother give;
60 She was a charmer, and could almost read
The thoughts of people: she told her, while she kept it,
'Twould make her amiable and subdue my father
Entirely to her love; but if she lost it
Or made a gift of it, my father's eye
65 Should hold her loathed, and his spirits should hunt
After new fancies: she, dying, gave it me;
And bid me, when my fate would have me wive,
To give it her. I did so: and take heed on't;
Make it a darling like your precious eye;
70 To lose't or give't away were such perdition
As nothing else could match.

DESDEMONA

Is't possible?

OTHELLO

'Tis true: there's magic in the web of it:
A sibyl, that had number'd in the world
75 The sun to course two hundred compasses,
In her prophetic fury sew'd the work;
The worms were hallow'd that did breed the silk;
And it was dy'd in mummy which the skillful
Conserv'd of maiden's hearts.

DESDEMONA

80　Indeed! is't true?

OTHELLO

Most veritable; therefore look to't well.

DESDEMONA

Then would to God that I had never seen't!

OTHELLO

Ha! wherefore?

DESDEMONA

Why do you speak so startingly and rash?

OTHELLO

85　Is't lost? is't gone? speak, is it out of the way?

DESDEMONA

Heaven bless us!

OTHELLO

Say you?

DESDEMONA

It is not lost; but what an if it were?

OTHELLO

How!

DESDEMONA

90　I say, it is not lost.

OTHELLO
Fetch't, let me see't.

DESDEMONA
Why, so I can, sir, but I will not now.
This is a trick to put me from my suit:
Pray you, let Cassio be receiv'd again.

OTHELLO
95 Fetch me the handkerchief: my mind misgives.

DESDEMONA
Come, come;
You'll never meet a more sufficient man.

OTHELLO
The handkerchief!

DESDEMONA
I pray, talk me of Cassio.

OTHELLO
100 The handkerchief!

DESDEMONA
A man that all his time
Hath founded his good fortunes on your love,
Shar'd dangers with you,—

OTHELLO
The handkerchief!

DESDEMONA

105   In sooth, you are to blame.

OTHELLO

Away!

[*Exit.*]

EMILIA

Is not this man jealous?

DESDEMONA

I ne'er saw this before.

Sure there's some wonder in this handkerchief;

110   I am most unhappy in the loss of it.

EMILIA

'Tis not a year or two shows us a man:

They are all but stomachs and we all but food:

They eat us hungerly, and when they are full,

They belch us.—Look you,—Cassio and my husband.

[*Enter* CASSIO *and* IAGO.]

IAGO

115   There is no other way; 'tis she must do't:

And, lo, the happiness! go and impórtune her.

DESDEMONA

How now, good Cassio! what's the news with you?

CASSIO

Madam, my former suit: I do beseech you
That by your virtuous means I may again
120   Exist, and be a member of his love,
Whom I, with all the office of my heart,
Entirely honour: I would not be delay'd.
If my offence be of such mortal kind
That nor my service past, nor present sorrows,
125   Nor purpos'd merit in futurity,
Can ransom me into his love again,
But to know so must be my benefit;
So shall I clothe me in a forc'd content,
And shut myself up in some other course,
130   To fortune's alms.

DESDEMONA

Alas, thrice-gentle Cassio!
My advocation is not now in tune;
My lord is not my lord; nor should I know him
Were he in favour as in humour alter'd.
135   So help me every spirit sanctified,
As I have spoken for you all my best,
And stood within the blank of his displeasure
For my free speech! You must awhile be patient:
What I can do I will; and more I will
140   Than for myself I dare: let that suffice you.

IAGO

Is my lord angry?

EMILIA

He went hence but now,

And certainly in strange unquietness.

IAGO
Can he be angry? I have seen the cannon,
145 When it hath blown his ranks into the air
And, like the devil, from his very arm
Puff'd his own brother;—and can he be angry?
Something of moment, then: I will go meet him:
There's matter in't indeed if he be angry.

DESDEMONA
150 I pr'ythee, do so.

[*Exit* **IAGO.**]

Something sure of state,—
Either from Venice or some unhatch'd practice
Made demonstrable here in Cyprus to him,—
Hath puddled his clear spirit, and in such cases
155 Men's natures wrangle with inferior things,
Though great ones are their object. 'Tis even so;
For let our finger ache, and it indues
Our other healthful members even to that sense
Of pain: nay, we must think men are not gods,
160 Nor of them look for such observancy
As fits the bridal.—Beshrew me much, Emilia,
I was,—unhandsome warrior as I am,—
Arraigning his unkindness with my soul;
But now I find I had suborn'd the witness,
165 And he's indicted falsely.

EMILIA

Pray heaven it be state matters, as you think,
And no conception nor no jealous toy
Concerning you.

DESDEMONA

Alas the day, I never gave him cause!

EMILIA

170 But jealous souls will not be answer'd so;
They are not ever jealous for the cause,
But jealous for they are jealous: 'tis a monster
Begot upon itself, born on itself.

DESDEMONA

Heaven keep that monster from Othello's mind!

EMILIA

175 Lady, amen.

DESDEMONA

I will go seek him.—Cassio, walk hereabout:
If I do find him fit, I'll move your suit,
And seek to effect it to my uttermost.

CASSIO

I humbly thank your ladyship.

[*Exeunt* **DESDEMONA** *and* **EMILIA**.]

[*Enter* **BIANCA**.]

BIANCA

180 Save you, friend Cassio!

CASSIO

What make you from home?
How is it with you, my most fair Bianca?
I'faith, sweet love, I was coming to your house.

BIANCA

And I was going to your lodging, Cassio.
185 What, keep a week away? seven days and nights?
Eight score eight hours? and lovers' absent hours,
More tedious than the dial eight score times?
O weary reckoning!

CASSIO

Pardon me, Bianca:
190 I have this while with leaden thoughts been press'd;
But I shall in a more continuate time
Strike off this score of absence. Sweet Bianca,

[*Giving her* **DESDEMONA'S** *handkerchief.*]

Take me this work out.

BIANCA

O Cassio, whence came this?
195 This is some token from a newer friend.
To the felt absence now I feel a cause:
Is't come to this? Well, well.

CASSIO

Go to, woman!

Throw your vile guesses in the devil's teeth,

200 From whence you have them. You are jealous now

That this is from some mistress, some remembrance:

No, in good troth, Bianca.

BIANCA

Why, whose is it?

CASSIO

I know not neither: I found it in my chamber.

205 I like the work well: ere it be demanded,—

As like enough it will,—I'd have it copied:

Take it, and do't; and leave me for this time.

BIANCA

Leave you! wherefore?

CASSIO

I do attend here on the general;

210 And think it no addition, nor my wish,

To have him see me woman'd.

BIANCA

Why, I pray you?

CASSIO

Not that I love you not.

BIANCA

But that you do not love me.

215 I pray you, bring me on the way a little;
And say if I shall see you soon at night.

CASSIO
'Tis but a little way that I can bring you,
For I attend here: but I'll see you soon.

BIANCA
'Tis very good; I must be circumstanc'd.

[*Exeunt.*]

ACT 4.

Scene 1. Cyprus. Before the Castle.

[Enter **Othello** *and* **Iago**.*]*

Iago
Will you think so?

Othello
Think so, Iago?

Iago
What,
To kiss in private?

Othello
5 An unauthoriz'd kiss.

Iago
Or to be naked with her friend in bed
An hour or more, not meaning any harm?

Othello
Naked in bed, Iago, and not mean harm!
It is hypocrisy against the devil:

10 They that mean virtuously and yet do so,
The devil their virtue tempts, and they tempt heaven.

IAGO

So they do nothing, 'tis a venial slip:
But if I give my wife a handkerchief,—

OTHELLO

What then?

IAGO

15 Why, then, 'tis hers, my lord, and being hers,
She may, I think, bestow't on any man.

OTHELLO

She is protectress of her honour too:
May she give that?

IAGO

Her honour is an essence that's not seen;
20 They have it very oft that have it not:
But, for the handkerchief,—

OTHELLO

By heaven, I would most gladly have forgot it:—
Thou said'st,—O, it comes o'er my memory,
As doth the raven o'er the infected house,
25 Boding to all,—he had my handkerchief.

IAGO

Ay, what of that?

OTHELLO

That's not so good now.

IAGO

What,

If I had said I had seen him do you wrong?

30 Or heard him say,—as knaves be such abroad,

Who having, by their own importunate suit,

Or voluntary dotage of some mistress,

Convincèd or supplied them, cannot choose

But they must blab,—

OTHELLO

35 Hath he said anything?

IAGO

He hath, my lord; but be you well assur'd,

No more than he'll unswear.

OTHELLO

What hath he said?

IAGO

Faith, that he did,—I know not what he did.

OTHELLO

40 What? what?

IAGO

Lie,—

OTHELLO
With her?

IAGO
With her, on her, what you will.

OTHELLO
Lie with her! lie on her!—We say lie on her when they belie
45 her.—Lie with her! that's fulsome.—Handkerchief—con-
fessions—handkerchief!—To confess, and be hanged for
his labour,—first, to be hanged, and then to confess.—I
tremble at it. Nature would not invest herself in such shad-
owing passion without some instruction. It is not words
50 that shake me thus:—pish!—noses, ears, and lips.—Is't
possible?—Confess,—handkerchief!—O devil!—

[*Falls in a trance.*]

IAGO
Work on,
My medicine, work! Thus credulous fools are caught;
And many worthy and chaste dames even thus,
55 All guiltless, meet reproach.—What, ho! my lord!
My lord, I say! Othello!

[*Enter* **CASSIO**.]

How now, Cassio!

CASSIO
What's the matter?

IAGO

My lord is fallen into an epilepsy:
60 This is his second fit; he had one yesterday.

CASSIO

Rub him about the temples.

IAGO

No, forbear;
The lethargy must have his quiet course:
If not, he foams at mouth, and by and by
65 Breaks out to savage madness. Look, he stirs:
Do you withdraw yourself a little while,
He will recover straight: when he is gone,
I would on great occasion speak with you.

[*Exit* CASSIO.]

How is it, general? have you not hurt your head?

OTHELLO

70 Dost thou mock me?

IAGO

I mock you! no, by heaven.
Would you would bear your fortune like a man!

OTHELLO

A hornèd man's a monster and a beast.

IAGO

There's many a beast, then, in a populous city,

75 And many a civil monster.

OTHELLO
Did he confess it?

IAGO
Good sir, be a man;
Think every bearded fellow that's but yok'd
May draw with you: there's millions now alive
80 That nightly lie in those unproper beds
Which they dare swear peculiar: your case is better.
O, 'tis the spite of hell, the fiend's arch-mock,
To lip a wanton in a secure couch,
And to suppose her chaste! No, let me know;
85 And knowing what I am, I know what she shall be.

OTHELLO
O, thou art wise; 'tis certain.

IAGO
Stand you awhile apart;
Confine yourself but in a patient list.
Whilst you were here o'erwhelmed with your grief,—
90 A passion most unsuiting such a man,—
Cassio came hither: I shifted him away,
And laid good 'scuse upon your ecstasy;
Bade him anon return, and here speak with me;
The which he promis'd. Do but encave yourself,
95 And mark the fleers, the gibes, and notable scorns,
That dwell in every region of his face;
For I will make him tell the tale anew,—
Where, how, how oft, how long ago, and when

He hath, and is again to cope your wife:
100 I say, but mark his gesture. Marry, patience;
Or I shall say you are all in all in spleen,
And nothing of a man.

OTHELLO
Dost thou hear, Iago?
I will be found most cunning in my patience;
105 But,—dost thou hear?—most bloody.

IAGO
That's not amiss;
But yet keep time in all. Will you withdraw?

[**OTHELLO** *withdraws.*]

Now will I question Cassio of Bianca,
A housewife that, by selling her desires,
110 Buys herself bread and clothes: it is a creature
That dotes on Cassio,—as 'tis the strumpet's plague
To beguile many and be beguil'd by one:—
He, when he hears of her, cannot refrain
From the excess of laughter:—here he comes:—
115 As he shall smile Othello shall go mad;
And his unbookish jealousy must construe
Poor Cassio's smiles, gestures, and light behavior
Quite in the wrong.

[*Re-enter* **CASSIO.**]

How do you now, lieutenant?

CASSIO

120   The worser that you give me the addition
Whose want even kills me.

IAGO

Ply Desdemona well, and you are sure on't.
[*Speaking lower.*] Now, if this suit lay in Bianca's power,
How quickly should you speed!

CASSIO

125   Alas, poor caitiff!

OTHELLO

[*Aside.*] Look, how he laughs already!

IAGO

I never knew a woman love man so.

CASSIO

Alas, poor rogue! I think, i'faith, she loves me.

OTHELLO

[*Aside.*] Now he denies it faintly and laughs it out.

IAGO

130   Do you hear, Cassio?

OTHELLO

Now he impórtunes him
To tell it o'er: go to; well said, well said.

IAGO

She gives it out that you shall marry her:
Do you intend it?

CASSIO

135   Ha, ha, ha!

OTHELLO

Do you triumph, Roman? do you triumph?

CASSIO

I marry her!—what? A customer! I pr'ythee, bear some
charity to my wit; do not think it so unwholesome:—ha,
ha, ha!

OTHELLO

140   So, so, so, so: they laugh that win.

IAGO

Faith, the cry goes that you shall marry her.

CASSIO

Pr'ythee, say true.

IAGO

I am a very villain else.

OTHELLO

Have you scored me? Well.

CASSIO

145 This is the monkey's own giving out: she is persuaded I
will marry her, out of her own love and flattery, not out
of my promise.

OTHELLO

Iago beckons me; now he begins the story.

CASSIO

She was here even now; she haunts me in every place. I was
150 the other day talking on the sea bank with certain Venetians,
and thither comes the bauble, and falls thus about my neck,—

OTHELLO

Crying, "O dear Cassio!" as it were: his gesture imports it.

CASSIO

So hangs, and lolls, and weeps upon me; so hales and pulls
me: ha, ha, ha!

OTHELLO

155 Now he tells how she plucked him to my chamber. O, I
see that nose of yours, but not that dog I shall throw it to.

CASSIO

Well, I must leave her company.

IAGO

Before me! look where she comes.

CASSIO

'Tis such another fitchew! marry, a perfumed one.

[Enter BIANCA.*]*

160   What do you mean by this haunting of me?

BIANCA
Let the devil and his dam haunt you! What did you mean
by that same handkerchief you gave me even now? I was
a fine fool to take it. I must take out the work?—A likely
piece of work that you should find it in your chamber and
165   not know who left it there! This is some minx's token, and
I must take out the work? There,—give it your hobby-
horse: wheresoever you had it, I'll take out no work on't.

CASSIO
How now, my sweet Bianca! how now! how now!

OTHELLO
By heaven, that should be my handkerchief!

BIANCA
170   An you'll come to supper to-night, you may; an you will
not, come when you are next prepared for.

[Exit.]

IAGO
After her, after her.

CASSIO
Faith, I must; she'll rail in the street else.

IAGO

Will you sup there?

CASSIO

175 Faith, I intend so.

IAGO

Well, I may chance to see you; for I would very fain speak with you.

CASSIO

Pr'ythee, come; will you?

IAGO

Go to; say no more.

[*Exit* CASSIO.]

OTHELLO

180 [*Coming forward.*] How shall I murder him, Iago?

IAGO

Did you perceive how he laughed at his vice?

OTHELLO

O Iago!

IAGO

And did you see the handkerchief?

OTHELLO

Was that mine?

IAGO

185 Yours, by this hand: and to see how he prizes the foolish woman your wife! she gave it him, and he hath given it his whore.

OTHELLO

I would have him nine years a-killing.—A fine woman! a fair woman! a sweet woman!

IAGO

190 Nay, you must forget that.

OTHELLO

Ay, let her rot, and perish, and be damned to-night; for she shall not live: no, my heart is turned to stone; I strike it, and it hurts my hand.—O, the world hath not a sweeter creature: she might lie by an emperor's side, and command him tasks.

IAGO

195 Nay, that's not your way.

OTHELLO

Hang her! I do but say what she is:—so delicate with her needle!—an admirable musician! O, she will sing the savageness out of a bear!—Of so high and plenteous wit and invention!—

IAGO

She's the worse for all this.

OTHELLO

200 O, a thousand, a thousand times:—and then, of so gentle a condition!

IAGO

Ay, too gentle.

OTHELLO

Nay, that's certain:—but yet the pity of it, Iago! O Iago, the pity of it, Iago!

IAGO

205 If you are so fond over her iniquity, give her patent to offend; for, if it touch not you, it comes near nobody.

OTHELLO

I will chop her into messes.—Cuckold me!

IAGO

O, 'tis foul in her.

OTHELLO

With mine officer!

IAGO

210 That's fouler.

OTHELLO

Get me some poison, Iago; this night.—I'll not expostulate with her, lest her body and beauty unprovide my mind again:—this night, Iago.

IAGO

Do it not with poison; strangle her in her bed, even the
215 bed she hath contaminated.

OTHELLO

Good, good: the justice of it pleases: very good.

IAGO

And for Cassio,—let me be his undertaker:—you shall hear more by midnight.

OTHELLO

Excellent good. [*A trumpet within.*] What trumpet is that 220 same?

IAGO

Something from Venice, sure. 'Tis Lodovico
Come from the duke: and, see, your wife is with him.

[*Enter* **LODOVICO**, **DESDEMONA**, *and* **ATTENDANTS**.]

LODOVICO

Save you, worthy general!

OTHELLO

With all my heart, sir.

LODOVICO

225 The duke and senators of Venice greet you.

[*Gives him a packet.*]

OTHELLO

I kiss the instrument of their pleasures.

[*Opens the packet and reads.*]

DESDEMONA

And what's the news, good cousin Lodovico?

IAGO

I am very glad to see you, signior;
Welcome to Cyprus.

LODOVICO

230 I thank you. How does Lieutenant Cassio?

IAGO

Lives, sir.

DESDEMONA

Cousin, there's fall'n between him and my lord
An unkind breach: but you shall make all well.

OTHELLO

Are you sure of that?

DESDEMONA

235 My lord?

OTHELLO

[*Reads.*] "This fail you not to do, as you will,—"

LODOVICO

He did not call; he's busy in the paper.
Is there division 'twixt my lord and Cassio?

DESDEMONA

A most unhappy one: I would do much

240 To atone them, for the love I bear to Cassio.

OTHELLO
Fire and brimstone!

DESDEMONA
My lord?

OTHELLO
Are you wise?

DESDEMONA
What, is he angry?

LODOVICO
245 May be the letter mov'd him;
For, as I think, they do command him home,
Deputing Cassio in his government.

DESDEMONA
Trust me, I am glad on't.

OTHELLO
Indeed!

DESDEMONA
250 My lord?

OTHELLO
I am glad to see you mad.

DESDEMONA
Why, sweet Othello,—

OTHELLO
Devil! [*Striking her.*]

DESDEMONA
I have not deserv'd this.

LODOVICO
255 My lord, this would not be believ'd in Venice,
Though I should swear I saw't: 'tis very much:
Make her amends; she weeps.

OTHELLO
O devil, devil!
If that the earth could teem with woman's tears,
260 Each drop she falls would prove a crocodile.—
Out of my sight!

DESDEMONA
I will not stay to offend you. [*Going.*]

LODOVICO
Truly, an obedient lady:—
I do beseech your lordship, call her back.

OTHELLO
265 Mistress!

DESDEMONA
My lord?

OTHELLO
What would you with her, sir?

LODOVICO
Who, I, my lord?

OTHELLO
Ay; you did wish that I would make her turn:
270 Sir, she can turn, and turn, and yet go on,
And turn again; and she can weep, sir, weep;
And she's obedient, as you say,—obedient,—
Very obedient.—Proceed you in your tears.—
Concerning this, sir,—O well-painted passion!
275 I am commanded home.—Get you away;
I'll send for you anon.—Sir, I obey the mandate,
And will return to Venice.—Hence, avaunt!

[*Exit* **DESDEMONA**.]

Cassio shall have my place. And, sir, to-night,
I do entreat that we may sup together:
280 You are welcome, sir, to Cyprus.—Goats and monkeys!

[*Exit.*]

LODOVICO
Is this the noble Moor whom our full senate
Call all-in-all sufficient? Is this the nature
Whom passion could not shake? whose solid virtue
The shot of accident nor dart of chance
285 Could neither graze nor pierce?

IAGO
He is much chang'd.

LODOVICO
Are his wits safe? is he not light of brain?

IAGO
He's that he is: I may not breathe my censure
What he might be,—if what he might he is not,—
290   I would to heaven he were!

LODOVICO
What, strike his wife!

IAGO
Faith, that was not so well; yet would I knew
That stroke would prove the worst!

LODOVICO
Is it his use?
295   Or did the letters work upon his blood,
And new-create this fault?

IAGO
Alas, alas!
It is not honesty in me to speak
What I have seen and known. You shall observe him;
300   And his own courses will denote him so
That I may save my speech: do but go after,
And mark how he continues.

LODOVICO
I am sorry that I am deceiv'd in him.

[*Exeunt.*]

SCENE 2. CYPRUS. A ROOM IN THE CASTLE.

[*Enter* **OTHELLO** *and* **EMILIA.**]

OTHELLO
You have seen nothing, then?

EMILIA
Nor ever heard, nor ever did suspect.

OTHELLO
Yes, you have seen Cassio and she together.

EMILIA
But then I saw no harm, and then I heard
5 Each syllable that breath made up between them.

OTHELLO
What, did they never whisper?

EMILIA
Never, my lord.

OTHELLO
Nor send you out o' the way?

EMILIA
Never.

OTHELLO
10 To fetch her fan, her gloves, her mask, nor nothing?

EMILIA
Never, my lord.

OTHELLO
That's strange.

EMILIA
I durst, my lord, to wager she is honest,
Lay down my soul at stake: if you think other,
15 Remove your thought,—it doth abuse your bosom.
If any wretch have put this in your head,
Let heaven requite it with the serpent's curse!
For if she be not honest, chaste, and true,
There's no man happy; the purest of their wives
20 Is foul as slander.

OTHELLO
Bid her come hither.—Go.

[*Exit* EMILIA.]

She says enough; yet she's a simple bawd
That cannot say as much. This is a subtle whore,
A closet-lock-and-key of villainous secrets:
25 And yet she'll kneel and pray; I have seen her do't.

[*Enter* EMILIA *with* DESDEMONA.]

DESDEMONA
My lord, what is your will?

OTHELLO
Pray, chuck, come hither.

DESDEMONA
What is your pleasure?

OTHELLO
Let me see your eyes;
30 Look in my face.

DESDEMONA
What horrible fancy's this?

OTHELLO
[*To* EMILIA.] Some of your function, mistress,
Leave procreants alone and shut the door;
Cough, or cry hem, if anybody come.
35 Your mystery, your mystery;—nay, despatch.

[*Exit* EMILIA.]

DESDEMONA
Upon my knees, what doth your speech import?
I understand a fury in your words,
But not the words.

OTHELLO
Why, what art thou?

DESDEMONA
40 Your wife, my lord; your true and loyal wife.

OTHELLO
Come, swear it, damn thyself;
Lest, being like one of heaven, the devils themselves
Should fear to seize thee: therefore be double-damn'd.—
Swear thou art honest.

DESDEMONA
45 Heaven doth truly know it.

OTHELLO
Heaven truly knows that thou art false as hell.

DESDEMONA
To whom, my lord? with whom? how am I false?

OTHELLO
O Desdemona!—away! away! away!

DESDEMONA
Alas the heavy day!—Why do you weep?
50 Am I the motive of these tears, my lord?
If haply you my father do suspect
An instrument of this your calling back,
Lay not your blame on me: if you have lost him,
Why, I have lost him too.

OTHELLO

55 Had it pleas'd heaven
To try me with affliction; had they rain'd
All kinds of sores and shames on my bare head;
Steep'd me in poverty to the very lips;
Given to captivity me and my utmost hopes;
60 I should have found in some place of my soul
A drop of patience: but, alas, to make me
A fixèd figure for the time, for scorn
To point his slow unmoving finger at!—
Yet could I bear that too; well, very well:
65 But there, where I have garner'd up my heart;
Where either I must live or bear no life,—
The fountain from the which my current runs,
Or else dries up; to be discarded thence!
Or keep it as a cistern for foul toads
70 To knot and gender in!—turn thy complexion there,
Patience, thou young and rose-lipp'd cherubin,—
Ay, there, look grim as hell!

DESDEMONA

I hope my noble lord esteems me honest.

OTHELLO

O, ay; as summer flies are in the shambles,
75 That quicken even with blowing. O thou weed,
Who art so lovely fair, and smell'st so sweet,
That the sense aches at thee,—would thou hadst ne'er
been born!

DESDEMONA

Alas, what ignorant sin have I committed?

OTHELLO

80 Was this fair paper, this most goodly book,
Made to write "whore" upon? What committed!
Committed!—O thou public commoner!
I should make very forges of my cheeks,
That would to cinders burn up modesty,
85 Did I but speak thy deeds.—What committed!
Heaven stops the nose at it, and the moon winks;
The bawdy wind, that kisses all it meets,
Is hush'd within the hollow mine of earth,
And will not hear it.—What committed!—
90 Impudent strumpet!

DESDEMONA

By heaven, you do me wrong.

OTHELLO

Are not you a strumpet?

DESDEMONA

No, as I am a Christian:
If to preserve this vessel for my lord
95 From any other foul unlawful touch
Be not to be a strumpet, I am none.

OTHELLO

What, not a whore?

DESDEMONA

No, as I shall be sav'd.

OTHELLO
Is't possible?

DESDEMONA
100 O, heaven forgive us!

OTHELLO
I cry you mercy then:
I took you for that cunning whore of Venice
That married with Othello.—You, mistress,
That have the office opposite to Saint Peter,
105 And keep the gate of hell!

[*Re-enter* **EMILIA**.]

You, you, ay, you!
We have done our course; there's money for your pains:
I pray you, turn the key, and keep our counsel.

[*Exit.*]

EMILIA
Alas, what does this gentleman conceive?—
110 How do you, madam? how do you, my good lady?

DESDEMONA
Faith, half asleep.

EMILIA
Good madam, what's the matter with my lord?

DESDEMONA

With who?

EMILIA

Why, with my lord, madam.

DESDEMONA

115   Who is thy lord?

EMILIA

He that is yours, sweet lady.

DESDEMONA

I have none: do not talk to me, Emilia;
I cannot weep; nor answer have I none
But what should go by water. Pr'ythee, to-night
120   Lay on my bed my wedding sheets,—remember;—
And call thy husband hither.

EMILIA

Here's a change indeed!

[*Exit.*]

DESDEMONA

'Tis meet I should be us'd so, very meet.
How have I been behav'd, that he might stick
125   The small'st opinion on my least misuse?

[*Re-enter* **EMILIA** *with* **IAGO**.]

IAGO

What is your pleasure, madam? How is't with you?

DESDEMONA

I cannot tell. Those that do teach young babes
Do it with gentle means and easy tasks:
He might have chid me so; for in good faith,
130 I am a child to chiding.

IAGO

What's the matter, lady?

EMILIA

Alas, Iago, my lord hath so bewhor'd her,
Thrown such despite and heavy terms upon her,
As true hearts cannot bear.

DESDEMONA

135 Am I that name, Iago?

IAGO

What name, fair lady?

DESDEMONA

Such as she says my lord did say I was.

EMILIA

He call'd her whore: a beggar in his drink
Could not have laid such terms upon his callet.

IAGO

140 Why did he so?

DESDEMONA

I do not know; I am sure I am none such.

IAGO

Do not weep, do not weep:—alas the day!

EMILIA

Hath she forsook so many noble matches,
Her father, and her country, and her friends,
145   To be call'd whore? would it not make one weep?

DESDEMONA

It is my wretched fortune.

IAGO

Beshrew him for't!
How comes this trick upon him?

DESDEMONA

Nay, heaven doth know.

EMILIA

150   I will be hang'd, if some eternal villain,
Some busy and insinuating rogue,
Some cogging, cozening slave, to get some office,
Have not devis'd this slander; I'll be hang'd else.

IAGO

Fie, there is no such man; it is impossible.

DESDEMONA

155   If any such there be, heaven pardon him!

EMILIA

A halter pardon him! and hell gnaw his bones!
Why should he call her whore? who keeps her company?
What place? what time? what form? what likelihood?
The Moor's abused by some most villainous knave,
160 Some base notorious knave, some scurvy fellow:—
O heaven, that such companions thou'dst unfold,
And put in every honest hand a whip
To lash the rascals naked through the world
Even from the east to the west!

IAGO

165 Speak within door.

EMILIA

O, fie upon them! some such squire he was
That turn'd your wit the seamy side without,
And made you to suspect me with the Moor.

IAGO

You are a fool; go to.

DESDEMONA

170 Alas, Iago,
What shall I do to win my lord again?
Good friend, go to him; for by this light of heaven,
I know not how I lost him. Here I kneel:—
If e'er my will did trespass 'gainst his love,
175 Either in discourse of thought or actual deed;
Or that mine eyes, mine ears, or any sense,
Delighted them in any other form;

Or that I do not yet, and ever did,
And ever will, though he do shake me off
180 To beggarly divorcement,—love him dearly,
Comfort forswear me! Unkindness may do much;
And his unkindness may defeat my life,
But never taint my love. I cannot say "whore,"—
It does abhor me now I speak the word;
185 To do the act that might the addition earn
Not the world's mass of vanity could make me.

IAGO

I pray you, be content; 'tis but his humour:
The business of the state does him offence,
And he does chide with you.

DESDEMONA
190 If 'twere no other,—

IAGO
'Tis but so, I warrant.

[*Trumpets within.*]

Hark, how these instruments summon to supper!
The messengers of Venice stay the meat:
Go in, and weep not; all things shall be well.

[*Exeunt* **DESDEMONA** *and* **EMILIA**.]

[*Enter* **RODERIGO**.]

195 How now, Roderigo!

RODERIGO

I do not find that thou dealest justly with me.

IAGO

What in the contrary?

RODERIGO

Every day thou daffest me with some device, Iago; and
rather, as it seems to me now, keepest from me all conve-
200 niency than suppliest me with the least advantage of hope.
I will indeed no longer endure it; nor am I yet persuaded
to put up in peace what already I have foolishly suffered.

IAGO

Will you hear me, Roderigo?

RODERIGO

Faith, I have heard too much; for your words and perfor-
205 mances are no kin together.

IAGO

You charge me most unjustly.

RODERIGO

With naught but truth. I have wasted myself out of my means.
The jewels you have had from me to deliver to Desdemona
would half have corrupted a votarist: you have told me she
210 hath received them, and returned me expectations and comforts of sudden respect and acquaintance; but I find none.

IAGO

Well; go to; very well.

RODERIGO

Very well! go to! I cannot go to, man; nor 'tis not very well: nay, I say 'tis very scurvy, and begin to find myself fobbed in it.

IAGO

215 Very well.

RODERIGO

I tell you 'tis not very well. I will make myself known to Desdemona: if she will return me my jewels, I will give over my suit and repent my unlawful solicitation; if not, assure yourself I will seek satisfaction of you.

IAGO

220 You have said now.

RODERIGO

Ay, and said nothing but what I protest intendment of doing.

IAGO

Why, now I see there's mettle in thee; and even from this instant do build on thee a better opinion than ever before. Give me thy hand, Roderigo. Thou hast taken against me

225 a most just exception; but yet, I protest, I have dealt most directly in thy affair.

RODERIGO

It hath not appeared.

IAGO

I grant indeed it hath not appeared, and your suspicion is not without wit and judgement. But, Roderigo, if thou hast

230   that in thee indeed, which I have greater reason to believe
now than ever,—I mean purpose, courage, and valour,—this
night show it: if thou the next night following enjoy not
Desdemona, take me from this world with treachery and
devise engines for my life.

RODERIGO

235   Well, what is it? is it within reason and compass?

IAGO

Sir, there is especial commission come from Venice to
depute Cassio in Othello's place.

RODERIGO

Is that true? why then Othello and Desdemona return
again to Venice.

IAGO

240   O, no; he goes into Mauritania, and takes away with him
the fair Desdemona, unless his abode be lingered here by
some accident: wherein none can be so determinate as the
removing of Cassio.

RODERIGO

How do you mean "removing" of him?

IAGO

245   Why, by making him uncapable of Othello's place;—
knocking out his brains.

RODERIGO

And that you would have me to do?

IAGO

Ay, if you dare do yourself a profit and a right. He sups
to-night with a harlotry, and thither will I go to him:—
250 he knows not yet of his honourable fortune. If you will
watch his going thence,—which I will fashion to fall out
between twelve and one,—you may take him at your pleasure: I will be near to second your attempt, and he shall fall
between us. Come, stand not amazed at it, but go along
255 with me; I will show you such a necessity in his death that
you shall think yourself bound to put it on him. It is now
high supper-time, and the night grows to waste: about it.

RODERIGO

I will hear further reason for this.

IAGO

And you shall be satisfied.

[*Exeunt.*]

SCENE 3. CYPRUS. ANOTHER ROOM IN THE CASTLE.

[*Enter* **OTHELLO, LODOVICO, DESDEMONA, EMILIA,** *and* **ATTENDANTS.**]

LODOVICO

I do beseech you, sir, trouble yourself no further.

OTHELLO

O, pardon me; 'twill do me good to walk.

LODOVICO

Madam, good night; I humbly thank your ladyship.

DESDEMONA
Your honour is most welcome.

OTHELLO
5   Will you walk, sir?—
O,—Desdemona,—

DESDEMONA
My lord?

OTHELLO
Get you to bed on the instant; I will be returned forthwith:
dismiss your attendant there: look't be done.

DESDEMONA
10 I will, my lord.

[*Exeunt* **OTHELLO**, **LODOVICO**, *and* **ATTENDANTS**.]

EMILIA
How goes it now? he looks gentler than he did.

DESDEMONA
He says he will return incontinent:
He hath commanded me to go to bed,
And bade me to dismiss you.

EMILIA
15 Dismiss me!

DESDEMONA
It was his bidding; therefore, good Emilia,

Give me my nightly wearing, and adieu:
We must not now displease him.

EMILIA

I would you had never seen him!

DESDEMONA

20 So would not I: my love doth so approve him,
That even his stubbornness, his checks, his frowns,—
Pr'ythee, unpin me,—have grace and favour in them.

EMILIA

I have laid those sheets you bade me on the bed.

DESDEMONA

All's one.—Good faith, how foolish are our minds!—
25 If I do die before thee, pr'ythee, shroud me
In one of those same sheets.

EMILIA

Come, come, you talk.

DESDEMONA

My mother had a maid call'd Barbara;
She was in love; and he she lov'd prov'd mad
30 And did forsake her: she had a song of "willow";
An old thing 'twas, but it express'd her fortune,
And she died singing it: that song to-night
Will not go from my mind; I have much to do
But to go hang my head all at one side,
35 And sing it like poor Barbara. Pr'ythee, despatch.

EMILIA
Shall I go fetch your night-gown?

DESDEMONA
No, unpin me here.—
This Lodovico is a proper man.

EMILIA
A very handsome man.

DESDEMONA
40 He speaks well.

EMILIA
I know a lady in Venice would have walked barefoot to
Palestine for a touch of his nether lip.

DESDEMONA

[*Sings.*]

"The poor soul sat sighing by a sycamore tree,
Sing all a green willow;
45 Her hand on her bosom, her head on her knee,
Sing willow, willow, willow:
The fresh streams ran by her, and murmur'd her moans;
Sing willow, willow, willow;
Her salt tears fell from her, and soften'd the stones;—"
50 Lay by these:—

[*Sings.*]

"Sing willow, willow, willow;—"
Pr'ythee, hie thee; he'll come anon:—

[*Sings.*]

"Sing all a green willow must be my garland.
Let nobody blame him; his scorn I approve,—"
55 Nay, that's not next.—Hark! who is't that knocks?

EMILIA
It's the wind.

DESDEMONA

[*Sings.*]

"I call'd my love false love; but what said he then?
Sing willow, willow, willow:
'If I court mo women, you'll couch with mo men.'"
60 So get thee gone; good night. Mine eyes do itch;
Doth that bode weeping?

EMILIA
'Tis neither here nor there.

DESDEMONA
I have heard it said so.—O, these men, these men!—
Dost thou in conscience think,—tell me, Emilia,—
65 That there be women do abuse their husbands
In such gross kind?

EMILIA
There be some such, no question.

DESDEMONA
Wouldst thou do such a deed for all the world?

EMILIA
Why, would not you?

DESDEMONA
70 No, by this heavenly light!

EMILIA
Nor I neither by this heavenly light; I might do't as well
i' the dark.

DESDEMONA
Wouldst thou do such a deed for all the world?

EMILIA
The world's a huge thing; it is a great price
75 For a small vice.

DESDEMONA
In troth, I think thou wouldst not.

EMILIA
In troth, I think I should; and undo't when I had done.
Marry, I would not do such a thing for a joint-ring, nor
for measures of lawn, nor for gowns, petticoats, nor caps,
80 nor any petty exhibition; but, for the whole world—why,

who would not make her husband a cuckold to make him
a monarch? I should venture purgatory for't.

DESDEMONA

Beshrew me, if I would do such a wrong for the whole world.

EMILIA

Why, the wrong is but a wrong i' the world; and having
85   the world for your labour, 'tis a wrong in your own world,
and you might quickly make it right.

DESDEMONA

I do not think there is any such woman.

EMILIA

Yes, a dozen; and as many to the vantage as would store
the world they play'd for.
90   But I do think it is their husbands' faults
If wives do fall: say that they slack their duties
And pour our treasures into foreign laps;
Or else break out in peevish jealousies,
Throwing restraint upon us; or say they strike us,
95   Or scant our former having in despite;
Why, we have galls; and though we have some grace,
Yet have we some revenge. Let husbands know
Their wives have sense like them: they see and smell
And have their palates both for sweet and sour,
100   As husbands have. What is it that they do
When they change us for others? Is it sport?
I think it is: and doth affection breed it?
I think it doth: is't frailty that thus errs?
It is so too. And have not we affections,

105 Desires for sport, and frailty, as men have?
Then let them use us well: else let them know
The ills we do their ills instruct us so.

DESDEMONA
Good-night, good-night: heaven me such usage send,
Not to pick bad from bad, but by bad mend!

[*Exeunt.*]

ACT 5.

Scene 1. Cyprus. A Street.

[*Enter* Iago *and* Roderigo.]

Iago
Here, stand behind this bulk; straight will he come:
Wear thy good rapier bare, and put it home:
Quick, quick; fear nothing; I'll be at thy elbow:
It makes us, or it mars us; think on that,
5   And fix most firm thy resolution.

Roderigo
Be near at hand; I may miscarry in't.

Iago
Here, at thy hand: be bold, and take thy stand.

[*Retires to a little distance.*]

Roderigo
I have no great devotion to the deed;
And yet he hath given me satisfying reasons:—
10   'Tis but a man gone.—Forth, my sword; he dies.

[Goes to his stand.]

IAGO
I have rubb'd this young quat almost to the sense,
And he grows angry. Now, whether he kill Cassio,
Or Cassio him, or each do kill the other,
Every way makes my gain: live Roderigo,
15 He calls me to a restitution large
Of gold and jewels that I bobb'd from him,
As gifts to Desdemona;
It must not be: if Cassio do remain,
He hath a daily beauty in his life
20 That makes me ugly; and besides, the Moor
May unfold me to him; there stand I in much peril;
No, he must die.—But, so, I hear him coming.

*[Enter **CASSIO**.]*

RODERIGO
I know his gait; 'tis he.—Villain, thou diest!

*[Rushes out, and makes a pass at **CASSIO**.]*

CASSIO
That thrust had been mine enemy indeed,
25 But that my coat is better than thou know'st:
I will make proof of thine.

*[Draws, and wounds **RODERIGO**.]*

RODERIGO
O, I am slain!

[**IAGO** *rushes from his post, cuts* **CASSIO** *behind in the leg, and exit.*]

CASSIO
I am maim'd forever.—Help, ho! murder! murder!

[*Falls.*]

[*Enter* **OTHELLO** *at a distance.*]

OTHELLO
The voice of Cassio: Iago keeps his word.

RODERIGO
30 O, villain that I am!

OTHELLO
It is even so.

CASSIO
O, help, ho! light! a surgeon!

OTHELLO
'Tis he:—O brave Iago, honest and just,
That hast such noble sense of thy friend's wrong!
35 Thou teachest me,—minion, your dear lies dead,
And your unbless'd fate hies. Strumpet, I come!
Forth of my heart those charms, thine eyes, are blotted;
Thy bed, lust-stain'd, shall with lust's blood be spotted.

[*Exit.*]

[*Enter* **LODOVICO** *and* **GRATIANO** *at a distance.*]

Cassio
What, ho! no watch? no passage? murder! murder!

Gratiano
40 'Tis some mischance; the cry is very direful.

Cassio
O, help!

Lodovico
Hark!

Roderigo
O wretched villain!

Lodovico
Two or three groan:—it is a heavy night:
45 These may be counterfeits: let's think't unsafe
To come in to the cry without more help.

Roderigo
Nobody come? then shall I bleed to death.

Lodovico
Hark!

[Re-enter **Iago**, *with a light.]*

Gratiano
Here's one comes in his shirt, with light and weapons.

IAGO

50   Who's there? whose noise is this that cries on murder?

LODOVICO

We do not know.

IAGO

Did not you hear a cry?

CASSIO

Here, here! for heaven's sake, help me!

IAGO

What's the matter?

GRATIANO

55   This is Othello's ancient, as I take it.

LODOVICO

The same indeed; a very valiant fellow.

IAGO

What are you here that cry so grievously?

CASSIO

Iago? O, I am spoil'd, undone by villains!
Give me some help.

IAGO

60   O me, lieutenant! what villains have done this?

CASSIO

I think that one of them is hereabout,
And cannot make away.

IAGO

O treacherous villains!—
[*To* **LODOVICO** *and* **GRATIANO**.] What are you there?
65   Come in and give some help.

RODERIGO

O, help me here!

CASSIO

That's one of them.

IAGO

O murderous slave! O villain!

[*Stabs* **RODERIGO**.]

RODERIGO

O damn'd Iago! O inhuman dog!

IAGO

70   Kill men i' the dark!—Where be these bloody thieves?—
How silent is this town!—Ho! murder! murder!—
What may you be? are you of good or evil?

LODOVICO

As you shall prove us, praise us.

IAGO
Signior Lodovico?

LODOVICO
75 He, sir.

IAGO
I cry you mercy. Here's Cassio hurt by villains.

GRATIANO
Cassio!

IAGO
How is't, brother?

CASSIO
My leg is cut in two.

IAGO
80 Marry, heaven forbid!—
Light, gentlemen:—I'll bind it with my shirt.

[*Enter* **BIANCA**.]

BIANCA
What is the matter, ho? who is't that cried?

IAGO
Who is't that cried!

BIANCA
O my dear Cassio, my sweet Cassio! O Cassio, Cassio, Cassio!

IAGO

85 O notable strumpet!—Cassio, may you suspect
Who they should be that have thus mangled you?

CASSIO

No.

GRATIANO

I am sorry to find you thus: I have been to seek you.

IAGO

Lend me a garter:—so.—O, for a chair,
90 To bear him easily hence!

BIANCA

Alas, he faints!—O Cassio, Cassio, Cassio!

IAGO

Gentlemen all, I do suspect this trash
To be a party in this injury.—
Patience awhile, good Cassio.—Come, come;
95 Lend me a light.—Know we this face or no?
Alas, my friend and my dear countryman
Roderigo? no:—yes, sure; O heaven! Roderigo.

GRATIANO

What, of Venice?

IAGO

Even he, sir: did you know him?

GRATIANO

100 Know him! ay.

IAGO

Signior Gratiano? I cry you gentle pardon;
These bloody accidents must excuse my manners,
That so neglected you.

GRATIANO

I am glad to see you.

IAGO

105 How do you, Cassio?—O, a chair, a chair!

GRATIANO

Roderigo!

IAGO

He, he, 'tis he.— [*A chair brought in.*] O, that's well
said;—the chair:—
Some good man bear him carefully from hence;
110 I'll fetch the general's surgeon. [*To* **BIANCA**.] For you, mistress,
Save you your labour.—He that lies slain here, Cassio,
Was my dear friend: what malice was between you?

CASSIO

None in the world; nor do I know the man.

IAGO

[*To* **BIANCA**.] What, look you pale?—O, bear him out o'
115 the air.

[CASSIO *and* RODERIGO *are borne off.*]

Stay you, good gentlemen.—Look you pale, mistress?—
Do you perceive the gastness of her eye?—
Nay, if you stare, we shall hear more anon.—
Behold her well; I pray you, look upon her:
120 Do you see, gentlemen? nay, guiltiness will speak
Though tongues were out of use.

[*Enter* EMILIA.]

EMILIA
'Las, what's the matter? what's the matter, husband?

IAGO
Cassio hath here been set on in the dark
By Roderigo, and fellows that are 'scap'd:
125 He's almost slain, and Roderigo dead.

EMILIA
Alas, good gentleman! alas, good Cassio!

IAGO
This is the fruit of whoring.—Pr'ythee, Emilia,
Go know of Cassio where he supp'd to-night.—
What, do you shake at that?

BIANCA
130 He supp'd at my house; but I therefore shake not.

IAGO
O, did he so? I charge you, go with me.

EMILIA
Fie, fie upon thee, strumpet!

BIANCA
I am no strumpet, but of life as honest
As you that thus abuse me.

EMILIA
135 As I! foh! fie upon thee!

IAGO
Kind gentlemen, let's go see poor Cassio dress'd.—
Come, mistress, you must tell's another tale.—
Emilia, run you to the citadel,
And tell my lord and lady what hath happ'd.—
140 Will you go on afore? [*Aside.*] This is the night
That either makes me or fordoes me quite.

[*Exeunt.*]

SCENE 2. CYPRUS. A BEDCHAMBER IN THE CASTLE: DESDEMONA IN BED ASLEEP; A LIGHT BURNING.

[*Enter* **OTHELLO.**]

OTHELLO
It is the cause, it is the cause, my soul,—
Let me not name it to you, you chaste stars!—
It is the cause.—Yet I'll not shed her blood;
Nor scar that whiter skin of hers than snow,
5 And smooth as monumental alabaster.

[Takes off his sword.]

That can thy light relume. When I have pluck'd thy rose,
I cannot give it vital growth again,
It must needs wither:—I'll smell it on the tree.—

[Kissing her.]

O, balmy breath, that dost almost persuade
10   Justice to break her sword!—One more, one more;—
Be thus when thou art dead, and I will kill thee,
And love thee after.—One more, and this the last;
So sweet was ne'er so fatal. I must weep,
But they are cruel tears: this sorrow's heavenly;
15   It strikes where it doth love.—She wakes.

DESDEMONA
Who's there? Othello?

OTHELLO
Ay, Desdemona.

DESDEMONA
Will you come to bed, my lord?

OTHELLO
Have you pray'd to-night, Desdemona?

DESDEMONA
20   Ay, my lord.

OTHELLO

If you bethink yourself of any crime
Unreconcil'd as yet to heaven and grace,
Solicit for it straight.

DESDEMONA

Alack, my lord, what may you mean by that?

OTHELLO

25 Well, do it, and be brief; I will walk by.
I would not kill thy unprepared spirit;
No,—heaven forfend!—I would not kill thy soul.

DESDEMONA

Talk you of killing?

OTHELLO

Ay, I do.

DESDEMONA

30 Then heaven have mercy on me!

OTHELLO

Amen, with all my heart!

DESDEMONA

If you say so, I hope you will not kill me.

OTHELLO

Hum!

DESDEMONA

And yet I fear you; for you are fatal then
35 When your eyes roll so: why I should fear I know not,
Since guiltiness I know not; but yet I feel I fear.

OTHELLO

Think on thy sins.

DESDEMONA

They are loves I bear to you.

OTHELLO

Ay, and for that thou diest.

DESDEMONA

40 That death's unnatural that kills for loving.—
Alas, why gnaw you so your nether lip?
Some bloody passion shakes your very frame:
These are portents; but yet I hope, I hope,
They do not point on me.

OTHELLO

45 Peace, and be still!

DESDEMONA

I will so. What's the matter?

OTHELLO

That handkerchief which I so loved and gave thee
Thou gav'st to Cassio.

DESDEMONA

No, by my life and soul!

50 Send for the man, and ask him.

OTHELLO

Sweet soul, take heed,

Take heed of perjury; thou'rt on thy death-bed.

DESDEMONA

Ay, but not yet to die.

OTHELLO

Yes, presently:

55 Therefore confess thee freely of thy sin;

For to deny each article with oath

Cannot remove nor choke the strong conception

That I do groan withal. Thou art to die.

DESDEMONA

Then, Lord have mercy on me!

OTHELLO

60 I say, amen.

DESDEMONA

And have you mercy too!—I never did

Offend you in my life; never lov'd Cassio

But with such general warranty of heaven

As I might love: I never gave him token.

OTHELLO

65 By heaven, I saw my handkerchief in 's hand.

O perjur'd woman! thou dost stone my heart,
And mak'st me call what I intend to do
A murder, which I thought a sacrifice:
I saw the handkerchief.

DESDEMONA

70 He found it then;
I never gave it him:—send for him hither;
Let him confess a truth.

OTHELLO

He hath confess'd.

DESDEMONA

What, my lord?

OTHELLO

75 That he hath us'd thee.

DESDEMONA

How? unlawfully?

OTHELLO

Ay.

DESDEMONA

He will not say so.

OTHELLO

No, his mouth is stopp'd;
80 Honest Iago hath ta'en order for't.

DESDEMONA

O, my fear interprets!—What, is he dead?

OTHELLO

Had all his hairs been lives, my great revenge
Had stomach for them all.

DESDEMONA

Alas, he is betray'd, and I undone!

OTHELLO

85 Out, strumpet! Weep'st thou for him to my face?

DESDEMONA

O, banish me, my lord, but kill me not!

OTHELLO

Down, strumpet!

DESDEMONA

Kill me to-morrow; let me live to-night!

OTHELLO

Nay, if you strive,—

DESDEMONA

90 But half an hour!

OTHELLO

Being done, there is no pause.

DESDEMONA
But while I say one prayer!

OTHELLO
It is too late.

[Smothers her.]

EMILIA
[*Within.*] My lord, my lord! what, ho! my lord, my lord!

OTHELLO
95 What noise is this?—Not dead? not yet quite dead?
I that am cruel am yet merciful;
I would not have thee linger in thy pain:—
So, so.

EMILIA
[*Within.*] What, ho! my lord, my lord!

OTHELLO
100 Who's there?

EMILIA
[*Within.*] O, good my lord, I would speak a word with you!

OTHELLO
Yes:—'tis Emilia:—by and by.—She's dead.—
'Tis like she comes to speak of Cassio's death;
The noise was high.—Ha! no more moving?
105 Still as the grave.—Shall she come in?—Were't good?—

I think she stirs again:—no.—What's best to do?
If she come in, she'll sure speak to my wife:
My wife! my wife! what wife? I have no wife.
O, insupportable! O heavy hour!
110 Methinks it should be now a huge eclipse
Of sun and moon, and that the affrighted globe
Should yawn at alteration.

EMILIA

[*Within.*] I do beseech you
That I may speak with you, O, good my lord!

OTHELLO

115 I had forgot thee: O, come in, Emilia:—
Soft,—by and by:—let me the curtains draw.—
Where art thou?

[*Unlocks the door.*]

[*Enter* **EMILIA**.]

What's the matter with thee now?

EMILIA

O, my good lord, yonder's foul murders done!

OTHELLO

120 What, now?

EMILIA

But now, my lord.

OTHELLO

It is the very error of the moon;
She comes more nearer earth than she was wont
And makes men mad.

EMILIA

125 Cassio, my lord, hath kill'd a young Venetian
Call'd Roderigo.

OTHELLO

Roderigo kill'd?
And Cassio kill'd?

EMILIA

No, Cassio is not kill'd.

OTHELLO

130 Not Cassio kill'd! then murder's out of tune,
And sweet revenge grows harsh.

DESDEMONA

O, falsely, falsely murder'd!

EMILIA

Alas, what cry is that?

OTHELLO

That! what?

EMILIA

135 Out, and alas! That was my lady's voice.—
Help! help, ho! help!—O lady, speak again!

Sweet Desdemona! O sweet mistress, speak!

DESDEMONA
A guiltless death I die.

EMILIA
O, who hath done this deed?

DESDEMONA
140 Nobody; I myself. Farewell:
Commend me to my kind lord: O, farewell!

[Dies.]

OTHELLO
Why, how should she be murder'd?

EMILIA
Alas, who knows?

OTHELLO
You heard her say herself it was not I.

EMILIA
145 She said so: I must needs report the truth.

OTHELLO
She's like a liar, gone to burning hell:
'Twas I that kill'd her.

EMILIA
O, the more angel she,

And you the blacker devil!

OTHELLO

150 She turn'd to folly, and she was a whore.

EMILIA

Thou dost belie her, and thou art a devil.

OTHELLO

She was false as water.

EMILIA

Thou art rash as fire, to say
That she was false: O, she was heavenly true!

OTHELLO

155 Cassio did tup her; ask thy husband else.
O, I were damn'd beneath all depth in hell,
But that I did proceed upon just grounds
To this extremity. Thy husband knew it all.

EMILIA

My husband!

OTHELLO

160 Thy husband.

EMILIA

That she was false to wedlock?

OTHELLO

Ay, with Cassio. Nay, had she been true,

184

If heaven would make me such another world
Of one entire and perfect chrysolite,
165 I'd not have sold her for it.

EMILIA
My husband!

OTHELLO
Ay, 'twas he that told me first:
An honest man he is, and hates the slime
That sticks on filthy deeds.

EMILIA
170 My husband!

OTHELLO
What needs this iterance, woman? I say thy husband.

EMILIA
O mistress, villainy hath made mocks with love!—
My husband say that she was false!

OTHELLO
He, woman;
175 I say thy husband: dost understand the word?
My friend, thy husband, honest, honest Iago.

EMILIA
If he say so, may his pernicious soul
Rot half a grain a day! he lies to the heart:
She was too fond of her most filthy bargain.

OTHELLO

180 Ha!

EMILIA

Do thy worst:
This deed of thine is no more worthy heaven
Than thou wast worthy her.

OTHELLO

Peace, you were best.

EMILIA

185 Thou hast not half that power to do me harm
As I have to be hurt. O gull! O dolt!
As ignorant as dirt! thou hast done a deed,—
I care not for thy sword; I'll make thee known,
Though I lost twenty lives.—Help! help, ho! help!
190 The Moor hath kill'd my mistress! murder, murder!

[*Enter* **MONTANO**, **GRATIANO**, *and* **IAGO**.]

MONTANO

What is the matter?—How now, general!

EMILIA

O, are you come, Iago? you have done well,
That men must lay their murders on your neck.

GRATIANO

What is the matter?

EMILIA

195 Disprove this villain, if thou be'st a man:
He says thou told'st him that his wife was false:
I know thou didst not, thou'rt not such a villain:
Speak, for my heart is full.

IAGO

I told him what I thought; and told no more
200 Than what he found himself was apt and true.

EMILIA

But did you ever tell him she was false?

IAGO

I did.

EMILIA

You told a lie; an odious, damnèd lie;
Upon my soul, a lie; a wicked lie:—
205 She false with Cassio!—Did you say with Cassio?

IAGO

With Cassio, mistress. Go to, charm your tongue.

EMILIA

I will not charm my tongue; I am bound to speak:
My mistress here lies murder'd in her bed,—

ALL

O heavens forfend!

EMILIA

210 And your reports have set the murder on.

OTHELLO

Nay, stare not, masters: it is true, indeed.

GRATIANO

'Tis a strange truth.

MONTANO

O monstrous act!

EMILIA

Villany, villany, villany!

215 I think upon't,—I think,—I smell't;—O villany!—
I thought so then;—I'll kill myself for grief:—
O villany, villany!

IAGO

What, are you mad? I charge you, get you home.

EMILIA

Good gentlemen, let me have leave to speak:

220 'Tis proper I obey him, but not now.—
Perchance, Iago, I will ne'er go home.

OTHELLO

O! O! O!

[Hanging over his wife.]

EMILIA

Nay, lay thee down and roar;
For thou hast kill'd the sweetest innocent
225 That e'er did lift up eye.

OTHELLO

[*Rising.*] O, she was foul!—
I scarce did know you, uncle; there lies your niece,
Whose breath, indeed, these hands have newly stopp'd:
I know this act shows horrible and grim.

GRATIANO

230 Poor Desdemona! I am glad thy father's dead:
Thy match was mortal to him, and pure grief
Shore his old thread in twain: did he live now,
This sight would make him do a desperate turn,
Yea, curse his better angel from his side,
235 And fall to reprobance.

OTHELLO

'Tis pitiful; but yet Iago knows
That she with Cassio hath the act of shame
A thousand times committed; Cassio confess'd it:
And she did gratify his amorous works
240 With that recognizance and pledge of love
Which I first gave her; I saw it in his hand:
It was a handkerchief, an antique token
My father gave my mother.

EMILIA

O heaven! O heavenly powers!

IAGO

245 Come, hold your peace.

EMILIA

'Twill out, 'twill out:—I peace!
No, I will speak as liberal as the north:
Let heaven and men and devils, let them all,
All, all, cry shame against me, yet I'll speak.

IAGO

250 Be wise, and get you home.

EMILIA

I will not.

[**IAGO** *offers to stab his wife.*]

GRATIANO

Fie!
Your sword upon a woman?

EMILIA

O thou dull Moor! that handkerchief thou speak'st of
255 I found by fortune and did give my husband;
For often with a solemn earnestness,—
More than, indeed, belong'd to such a trifle,—
He begg'd of me to steal it.

IAGO

Villanous whore!

EMILIA

260 She give it Cassio! no, alas, I found it,
And I did give't my husband.

IAGO

Filth, thou liest!

EMILIA

By heaven, I do not, I do not, gentlemen.—
O murderous coxcomb! What should such a fool
265 Do with so good a wife?

OTHELLO

Are there not stones in heaven
But what serve for thunder?—Precious villain!

[IAGO *stabs* EMILIA, *and then runs out.*]

GRATIANO

The woman falls; sure, he hath kill'd his wife.

EMILIA

Ay, ay:—O, lay me by my mistress' side.

GRATIANO

270 He's gone, but his wife's kill'd.

MONTANO

'Tis a notorious villain. Take you this weapon,
Which I have here recover'd from the Moor:
Come, guard the door without; let him not pass,

But kill him rather. I'll after that same villain,
275 For 'tis a damnèd slave.

[*Exit* MONTANO *and* GRATIANO.]

OTHELLO
I am not valiant neither,
But every puny whipster gets my sword:—
But why should honour outlive honesty?
Let it go all.

EMILIA
280 What did thy song bode, lady?
Hark, canst thou hear me? I will play the swan,
And die in music:—

[*Sings.*]

"Willow, willow, willow."
Moor, she was chaste; she lov'd thee, cruel Moor;
285 So come my soul to bliss, as I speak true;
So speaking as I think, I die,—I die.

[*Dies.*]

OTHELLO
I have another weapon in this chamber;
It is a sword of Spain, the ice-brook's temper:—
O, here it is.—Uncle, I must come forth.

GRATIANO
290 [*Within.*] If thou attempt it, it will cost thee dear:

Thou hast no weapon, and perforce must suffer.

OTHELLO

Look in upon me then, and speak with me,
Or, naked as I am, I will assault thee.

[*Re-enter* **GRATIANO.**]

GRATIANO

What is the matter?

OTHELLO

295 Behold, I have a weapon;
A better never did itself sustain
Upon a soldier's thigh: I have seen the day
That with this little arm and this good sword
I have made my way through more impediments
300 Than twenty times your stop:—but, O vain boast!
Who can control his fate? 'tis not so now.—
Be not afraid, though you do see me weapon'd;
Here is my journey's end, here is my butt,
And very sea-mark of my utmost sail.
305 Do you go back dismay'd? 'tis a lost fear;
Man but a rush against Othello's breast,
And he retires:—where should Othello go?—
Now, how dost thou look now? O ill-starr'd wench!
Pale as thy smock! When we shall meet at compt,
310 This look of thine will hurl my soul from heaven,
And fiends will snatch at it. Cold, cold, my girl!
Even like thy chastity.—
O cursèd, cursèd slave!—Whip me, ye devils,
From the possession of this heavenly sight!

315 Blow me about in winds! roast me in sulphur!
Wash me in steep-down gulfs of liquid fire!—
O Desdemon! dead, Desdemon! dead! O!

[*Enter* **Lodovico**, **Montano**, **Cassio** *carried in a chair, and* **Officers**
with **Iago** *prisoner.*]

Lodovico
Where is this rash and most unfortunate man?

Othello
That's he that was Othello;—here I am.

Lodovico
320 Where is that viper? bring the villain forth.

Othello
I look down towards his feet;—but that's a fable.—
If that thou be'st a devil, I cannot kill thee.

[*Wounds* **Iago.**]

Lodovico
Wrench his sword from him.

Iago
I bleed, sir, but not kill'd.

Othello
325 I am not sorry neither: I'd have thee live;
For, in my sense, 'tis happiness to die.

LODOVICO

O thou Othello, that wert once so good,
Fall'n in the practice of a damnèd slave,
What shall be said to thee?

OTHELLO

330 Why, anything;
An honourable murderer, if you will;
For naught did I in hate, but all in honour.

LODOVICO

This wretch hath part confess'd his villany:
Did you and he consent in Cassio's death?

OTHELLO

335 Ay.

CASSIO

Dear general, I never gave you cause.

OTHELLO

I do believe it, and I ask your pardon.
Will you, I pray, demand that demi-devil
Why he hath thus ensnar'd my soul and body?

IAGO

340 Demand me nothing: what you know, you know:
From this time forth I never will speak word.

LODOVICO

What, not to pray?

GRATIANO
Torments will ope your lips.

OTHELLO
Well, thou dost best.

LODOVICO
345 Sir, you shall understand what hath befall'n,
Which, as I think, you know not. Here is a letter
Found in the pocket of the slain Roderigo,
And here another: the one of them imports
The death of Cassio to be undertook
350 By Roderigo.

OTHELLO
O villain!

CASSIO
Most heathenish and most gross!

LODOVICO
Now here's another discontented paper,
Found in his pocket too; and this, it seems,
355 Roderigo meant to have sent this damnèd villain;
But that, belike, Iago in the interim
Came in and satisfied him.

OTHELLO
O the pernicious caitiff!—
How came you, Cassio, by that handkerchief
360 That was my wife's?

CASSIO

I found it in my chamber;
And he himself confess'd but even now
That there he dropp'd it for a special purpose
Which wrought to his desire.

OTHELLO

365 O fool! fool! fool!

CASSIO

There is besides in Roderigo's letter,—
How he upbraids Iago, that he made him
Brave me upon the watch; whereon it came
That I was cast: and even but now he spake,
370 After long seeming dead,—Iago hurt him,
Iago set him on.

LODOVICO

You must forsake this room, and go with us:
Your power and your command is taken off,
And Cassio rules in Cyprus. For this slave,—
375 If there be any cunning cruelty
That can torment him much and hold him long,
It shall be his. You shall close prisoner rest,
Till that the nature of your fault be known
To the Venetian state.—Come, bring away.

OTHELLO

380 Soft you; a word or two before you go.
I have done the state some service, and they know't.—
No more of that.—I pray you, in your letters,
When you shall these unlucky deeds relate,

Speak of me as I am; nothing extenuate,
385 Nor set down aught in malice: then must you speak
Of one that loved not wisely, but too well;
Of one not easily jealous, but, being wrought,
Perplex'd in the extreme; of one whose hand,
Like the base Judean, threw a pearl away
390 Richer than all his tribe; of one whose subdu'd eyes,
Albeit unusèd to the melting mood,
Drop tears as fast as the Arabian trees
Their medicinal gum. Set you down this;
And say besides,—that in Aleppo once,
395 Where a malignant and a turban'd Turk
Beat a Venetian and traduc'd the state,
I took by the throat the circumcisèd dog
And smote him—thus.

[*Stabs himself.*]

LODOVICO
O bloody period!

GRATIANO
400 All that's spoke is marr'd.

OTHELLO
I kiss'd thee ere I kill'd thee:—no way but this,
Killing myself, to die upon a kiss. [*Falling upon* **DESDEMONA**.]

CASSIO
This did I fear, but thought he had no weapon;
For he was great of heart.

LODOVICO

405   [*To* IAGO.] O Spartan dog,
      More fell than anguish, hunger, or the sea!
      Look on the tragic loading of this bed;
      This is thy work:—the object poisons sight;
      Let it be hid.—Gratiano, keep the house,
410   And seize upon the fortunes of the Moor,
      For they succeed on you.—To you, lord governor,
      Remains the censure of this hellish villain;
      The time, the place, the torture,—O, enforce it!
      Myself will straight aboard; and to the state
415   This heavy act with heavy heart relate.

                  [*Exeunt.*]

ABOUT THE AUTHOR

William Shakespeare (1564–1616) was born in Stratford-upon-Avon, Warwickshire, to a middle-class glover and landowner's daughter. He married Anne Hathaway in 1582 and moved to London to work with a theatrical troupe ten years later.

Since little has been learned of his early life, nearly all of what we know about Shakespeare begins—on the London stage—in 1592. In the wake of his critical and public success, Shakespeare helped build the Globe theater on the River Thames.

Regarded as the world's preeminent dramatist, his extant works include thirty-eight plays, one hundred and fifty-four sonnets, and two narrative poems, and have been translated into every major language. To this day, his plays have been performed more often than those of any other playwright—adapted for film and television, updated, deconstructed, and transfigured into ballets, operas, and musicals. Though his formal education exceeded no further than grammar school, William Shakespeare became the most transcendent and influential writer in all of world literature.